N. ARNOLD

CUSTOMS AND COOKERY
in the
Périgord and Quercy

CUSTOMS AND COOKERY
in the
Périgord and Quercy

ANNE PENTON
Drawings by Robert Geary

DAVID & CHARLES : NEWTON ABBOT

For E.A.J.D.

0 7153 6111 2

© Anne Penton 1973

Set in 11 on 13 point Baskerville
and printed in Great Britain
by W J Holman Limited Dawlish
for David & Charles (Holdings) Limited
South Devon House Newton Abbot Devon

CONTENTS

Chapter One

THE PROVINCE

THE Périgord is a country of contrasts, of châteaux and grottoes, gently wooded rolling landscape interspersed with streams and rivers bordered by poplars and wide panoramic views of the north, but changing in character further south or to the east or west. To the west, the road through the Dordogne to Libourne and Bordeaux passes through the Forêt de la Double. There are lakes here where, in the summer, people go to fish and to swim, and from the main road smaller ones lead to tiny villages hidden by the trees, until the first houses emerge in the clearings from the shade of the forest, dazzling in the sunlight. To the south and east, the country takes on a different aspect: the east, bordered by the Limousin and the Massif Central Departments, is wooded with valleys in the north, but further south begin the dry limestone plateaux, so characteristic of the Quercy.

The Périgord is divided into the Périgord Blanc above Périgeux, and the Périgord Noir below. It is easy to see why, for in the southern half the country is more thickly wooded, with dark pines, chestnuts and oak trees predominating. The hills are craggier and more sharply defined, with rocks and boulders on the plateaux and in the forests. This is the region of the pre-historic painted caves of Lascaux and the Font de Gaume, and of the grottoes, with stalagmite and stalactite formations, such as the grotto with the Virgin at Domme, an ancient town built of honey-coloured stone perched high on a rock commanding a magnificent view of the Dordogne Valley and its castles; and of Le Grand Roc at Les Eyzies, which is ringed by grey lime-stone cliffs pitted with caves and grottoes, many still unexplored.

Part of an old village in the Périgord

All over this ancient province, dating back to the Renaissance and earlier, are the châteaux. Indeed, the Périgord is known as the country of a thousand castles. They stand on the hills guard-ing the towns and villages, overlooking the rivers or screened by the trees, proud and beautiful, reminders of France's rich and turbulent past.

The Quercy and the Périgord Agenais, of which Villeneuve

8

sur Lot is the centre, have certain geographical similarities with the Périgord and yet they are very different. The north-east of the Quercy, known as La Chataigneraie, is cold and wet, with poor soil. Formerly only buckwheat and rye grew here, though now, thanks to river diversion and more modern agricultural techniques, wheat, root crops and fruit trees are cultivated. The Celé, Cère and Lot rivers flow through the plateau in deep gorges between high cliffs of golden and pink rock. The Chataigneraie is divided from that part of the province known as the Haut Quercy by a fertile plain, the Limargue, of which the most important town is Figeac, once an important staging post on the pilgrimage route across France down to St James of Compostella in Spain. The Haut Quercy is mysterious and wild country, formed in large parts of limestone plateaux known as Causses, through which pass the Dordogne and the Lot.

The most important of these Causses, of which there are three, is the Causse de Gramat, between the two rivers. Although it is dry and arid on the surface, underground rivers and streams flow through it, forming caverns and galleries like those at Padirac, which are visited by boat. Little grows here except trees and scrub, and the vast stony plateau, crisscrossed by low stone walls, has an inhospitable air. One can go for miles without meeting a soul, the only signs of life being the birds, sometimes a rabbit or hare, or a flock of the sheep known as 'bespectacled' because of the black rings round their eyes. These sheep are to be seen also on the Causse de Martel, which is similar to Gramat with its grey stone and its walls built by the shepherds in vain attempts to clear their land and fence in the sheep.

Yet these Causses and the Haut Quercy offer much to see. As one crosses the Causse de Gramat, the extraordinary canyon of Rocamadour with its shrines and churches climbing the cliff suddenly appears. Home of the Black Virgin, and a pilgrimage centre from the time of the Middle Ages, it gives the feeling of having been here since the beginning of time, its caves inhabited by our earliest ancestors to shelter from the harshness of the climate and nature. The road from Cahors to Figeac running along the Valley of the Lot also has its peculiar charm. This is no broad, flat valley; on the contrary, the river is closed in and flanked by cliffs ranging in colour from ochre to black, on top of which are perched castles such as that of Cenevières, overhanging the river, and with villages built up the escarpments, such as St-Cirq-Lapopie with its ruined castle and its great Gothic church at the top. Next to Rocamadour, it is known as the second wonder of the Lot.

But if one drives on the small roads away from the tourist spots and into the heart of the country, through the wooded hills flanking the Causses and rising up from the river valleys, one is aware of a sense of timelessness. I lost my way one day when going to visit a baker whose address had been given me in a little village on the edge of the Causse de Gramat. No one passed me as I drove up the narrow road winding its way to the top of the hill. Here was a crossroads, with no sign in any direction. Guessing, I drove on through the woods until I came to a tiny village in a small valley. The houses were grouped round a square; half of them seemed abandoned and nobody was about. Then I saw the café. Inside, a very old lady and her middle-aged daughter were preparing their midday meal in the kitchen, which also served as their living room and the bar. Talking to them, I discovered that I was not very far away from where I wished to go, but neither of them had ever been there. The old lady had never been out of her village. She had been born there and married in the little church round the corner, and no doubt would be buried in the graveyard next to it. And were those houses abandoned? How many inhabitants were there?

'Ah, Mademoiselle,' the daughter replied, 'the village is dying. There are no young here. It is many years since we had a birth and a christening, and when someone dies, his house falls into ruins. But we who remain live exactly as our parents and grand-parents did. Nothing changes here.'

The Périgord Agenais is that part of south-west France which is now the Lot and Garonne Department, adjacent to the Quercy and south of the Périgord. Consequently it has characteristics of both the wild savage country of the Lot and the green hills and valleys of the Dordogne. It is a fertile land, which gives one the impression of an immense orchard; for what strike one immediately after leaving the slopes of the south of the Périgord are the acres of fruit trees—pears, peaches and above all, plum trees. Collected and dried out in oval-shaped containers in specially constructed ovens, Agen prunes enjoy a world-wide reputation. But talk to anybody in the thirteenth-century fortified town of Villeneuve sur Lot and he will tell you that this is a misnomer. Villeneuve is the centre of the prune industry, and the best prunes are Villeneuvois, grown and dried in the villages sur-rounding the town; no one should leave this picturesque town without going into the sweet and pastry shops and tasting or buying their prunes stuffed with almond paste, packed invitingly in little violet boxes.

The whole of this region, the Périgord, the Périgord Agenais and the Quercy, is one with an immensely varied history, fought over by the English and French in the days when it formed part of the Angevin Empire and during the Hundred Years' War. Evidence of its troubled past survives in the numerous fortified towns or Bastides, as they are called, such as Monpazier in the Dordogne, Monflanquin and Villeneuve sur Lot, in the fortified Romanesque churches and in the names of villages like Le Pas de l'Anglais. Its inhabitants have figured in French history and culture throughout the centuries. This is the country of Mon-taigne and his great friend La Boetie, whose beautiful house can still be seen at Sarlat, of theologians like Fénélon, one-time tutor to the Duc de Bourgogne, son of Louis XIV. The painter Ingres was born in Montauban in the south of the Quercy, where a

11

museum, situated in the old episcopal palace, contains a large collection of his work. Politically, two great names stand out: no one can visit Cahors, capital of the Lot, without becoming aware of its two most important sons—Pope John XXII and Leon Gambetta, the man who left Paris in a balloon during the 1871 siege in an attempt to rally the people from Tours, and who was one of the founders of the Third Republic. And in the north-west of the Périgord, at Chalais, large estates were owned by the family of Monsieur l'Abbé de Périgord, so prominent a Frenchman under his more famous name of Talleyrand.

Although neither the Périgord, the Quercy nor the Agenais is technically in the south of France, and the inhabitants will take great pride in confirming this, certain of the southern characteristics appear soon after one enters the area from the north. Already one is aware of that peculiar brilliancy of light so typical of Provence and the Languedoc, and so often captured on canvas by the Impressionists. In the spring and summer the sky is a more intense blue and the rays of the sun are stronger. The houses, too, are more akin to those of the south: gone are the dark slate roofs of the Touraine, and instead the red tiles of the Midi glow in the sunlight. Built of grey or honey coloured stone, there is great architectural variety among them. Long and low in the north, with dovecotes under the eaves and vines and roses overhanging the doors and windows, the houses change radically in the southern half of the Périgord and in the Quercy. Here they have two storeys with steps leading up to the first. Often there is a small stone terrace with vines or creeper climbing up the columns and overhanging it. Many of these houses have square towers, topped with pointed tiled roofs—the pigeon-cotes of former days, now often used for storing the maize for the poultry and cattle.

Inside the old farmhouses the kitchens are light and airy, with wooden ceilings and scrubbed wood or stone flagged floors. In the corners the huge round-bellied grandfather clocks, their cases painted with flowers or birds, tick comfortably away. Every kitchen has its oak dresser, with a closed-in top, and many of them are richly carved. On the shelves stand the jars filled with goose, duck and pork fat, yellow maize flour and the little pickled cucumbers to eat with the pâtés, cold meats and pot au feu. But

Part of the living room of a Dordogne farmhouse

what immediately draw the eye as one enters these kitchens are the large fireplaces with high stone chimneys. Though picturesque, many of them are primitively constructed and tend to smoke badly. To overcome this, brightly patterned strips of material about a foot deep are suspended across the bottom of

13

the mantelpiece to draw up the smoke into the chimney. Much of the cooking is still done on these fires, on iron grills or in large cast-iron pots standing in the embers or suspended from hooks set into the chimney. Although modern cookers now supplement the open fire, the old tradition of wood-fired ovens has not died out. In the old days, when a dish had to be baked it was carried to the oven in the bakehouse in the yard, or to the village baker's to be cooked there after the bread. Nowadays, a separate oven fired with logs stands by the cooker to fulfil this purpose, and also to heat the upstairs of the house in winter.

To many, apart from its castles, caves and grottoes, the Périgord is synonymous with the pleasures of the table. And rightly so. But gastronomically the Quercy cannot be separated from the Périgord; for both these old provinces produce the truffle—the black diamond—eulogised by countless writers and poets. Curnonsky, the celebrated French gastronome, called it the 'perfumed soul' of the Périgord. Which province produces the better one, the blacker and the more highly scented? Talk to a Périgourdin and he will contemptuously dismiss those which come from the Lot, saying that the flavour is less fine and the scent not so powerful. Then go and ask a Quercynois the same question—as I did once. He laughed, saying they were both equally fine, and then added, 'But what the Périgourdins don't always realise is that of those truffles they take to be their own in the markets and which they praise so highly to the detriment of ours, quite a high proportion come from our Causses and our oaks. But don't tell them I told you, for they would never believe it.'

From this region and from the Périgord Agenais comes the foie gras of specially fattened geese and ducks which rivals that of Strasburg, and which some connoisseurs judge superior. As one goes through the towns, the signs outside the *charcuteries* depict big fat geese with 'foie gras' written underneath instead of the rosy smiling pigs seen elsewhere in France. These geese

14

and ducks are *gavés* (stuffed) on boiled maize for a month to three weeks before being killed, and are then preserved in their own fat and stored in large stone jars, their livers, weighing up to two pounds or more sometimes, turned into foie gras, or mixed with pork for other pâtés. For here too, the pig (and every farmer keeps some) plays a supreme role in the cooking. Every part of the animal is used: in the black and white puddings, in

Le gavage: *fattening the table birds by stuffing them with maize*

sausages and pâtés, in stews and soups. The rind, if it is not used fresh to enrich sauces and stews, is preserved rolled up in little parcels in its own fat, and then eaten in soups or with vegetables as an entrée. Some of the loveliest dishes in the whole repertoire of the local cooking are made from some part of the pig, such as the Enchaud de Porc, which is either liberally truffled for special

15

occasions or more simply flavoured with garlic, or liver, stuffed with truffles and herbs and braised in white wine with tiny onions. Apart from these, pork is used in stuffings for vegetables and also goes into fish dishes, and as well as the goose and duck fat, or the walnut oil, pork fat is the basis of the cooking. Butter is used very little except for certain types of cakes and pastry, though it is sometimes eaten with the radishes and salamé that constitute part of the hors d'oeuvres, or for breakfast.

The local cooking, however, does not consist only of truffles, duck and goose livers, preserved poultry and pork products. Maize is cultivated extensively, not only for the *gavage* (the fattening of birds) or for feeding the cattle during the winter months, but for its flour, which used to be baked into big flat round loaves and is now made into dumplings, pancakes and other sweets. Game too is plentiful, especially partridges, pheasants and hares—these last being stuffed and roasted, or cooked in rich dark sauces. The rivers and streams abound with trout, pike, perch and other freshwater fish, including the *écrevisse*— the little freshwater crayfish which used to be eaten at special picnics in England, but which no one bothers to catch any more.

Apart from a few industries, this whole region is still predominantly agricultural and most of the people work on the land. Even the artisans, blacksmiths and builders have their patches of land outside the villages where they grow vegetables and flowers. Every farmer's wife has a well-stocked kitchen garden, where rows of tiny peas, beans of all variety, lettuces, radishes, garlic and carrots stand close together. At the far end are the tomato plants, the currant bushes and the strawberry beds, whilst all over the farm are to be found the walnut and fruit trees—cherry, plum, peach and fig, the last heavy in September with those green figs whose pink and golden flesh—for those who like them —tastes of honey, or with the dark red and purple varieties which ripen in October.

The vegetables are eaten as young as possible, or bottled

whilst still young. On rainy days and in the evenings, after the animals have been fed and cared for, it is quite a common sight to see the steriliser bubbling away on a trivet over the fire in the kitchen. Not for these people the frozen pea or artificially coloured green bean, nor would they look kindly on tinned fruit in a synthetic-tasting syrup. If not eaten straight away, the fruit is made into jams and jellies, into syrups to dilute with ice and water for summer drinks, or into liqueurs; or it is preserved in eau-de-vie to be eaten in small glasses with a little of the juice as a digestif after the copious Sunday lunches.

Throughout the year, therefore, a housewife of this region is busily preserving what cannot be used at the time. If she lives on a farm she often rises between five and six am, and in addition to running the house, tending the kitchen garden, poultry, pigs and rabbits, which are her responsibility, and milking the cows, she takes her produce to sell in the local market. She also helps her husband in the fields, unlike the women in some departments further north who stay at home. As one woman said to me, it never seems to stop. Yet these people are some of the most cheerful, hospitable and helpful I know. Should you call on them, no matter at what time of day or what they are doing, you will automatically be offered refreshment—a glass of wine, or some *cassis* (that delicious blackcurrant liqueur), or perhaps some cherries or plums preserved in eau-de-vie. How often I must have been silently cursed by my neighbours or other friends when I appeared at odd times of day or in the evenings, to ask some small service or to find out the best way of dealing with a recipe I had just come across and wished to try out. And how stupid and ignorant I must have appeared when I enquired more particularly as to quantities of ingredients and timing:

'For the stuffing, you take *un quart* of minced veal.'

'But, Madame, isn't a quarter of a kilo rather a lot, considering the rest of the ingredients?'

'I mean 125 grammes, a quarter of a *livre*.'

And the *livre* does not correspond exactly to the pound weight either.

Or:

'Bake in the oven until it is done.'

'For how long and in how hot an oven?'

'Oh, about half an hour in a fairly hot oven; but sometimes you have to allow more and sometimes I find it is cooked before that time, particularly if my oven is very hot.'

Timing and regulating log-fired ovens and gas ones are two different things. Cooking, for these people, is a matter of memory from having watched their mothers, experience and *feel*. But it works for them, for they are born cooks with a long tradition of good food behind them which they are carrying on.

That the inhabitants of this region take their food seriously is evident from their appearance. One has only to see them on market days, as they gather together for their *café cognacs*, to realise that food is not a subject lightly to be dismissed. Dark, with brown skins, red cheeks and very fine eyes, many of them are stockily built and tend to put on weight early in life. But this is nothing to be ashamed of, as I found when complimenting, as I thought, a local friend on having lost weight. He was highly insulted, taking my remarks as a slur on his wife's cooking. And one may be sure, as these farmers sit there in the cafés, dressed in their dark suits and berets, that as well as catching up on the latest gossip and arguing about local politics, they will turn to food and drink in one form or another as a subject of earnest discussion.

Accustomed as most of us are today to two, three or at the most four courses, the French can seem to have large appetites. At one Sunday lunch to which I was invited, we worked our way through soup, hors d'oeuvres of various pâtés, sausages garnished with hard-boiled eggs, slices of melon with the local cured ham and a beetroot and onion salad, a civet of hare garnished with fried bread croutons, roast chicken with *cèpes* (the local mushrooms),

18

a dish of tiny green beans, salad and cheese. A home-made coffee ice with petit fours completed the meal before coffee and liqueurs. Such a meal would not be served for lunch on week-days, but no meal includes less than four or five courses, and the first is always soup, which is also served at the evening meal.

'If my wife didn't serve up soup twice a day I wouldn't be happy,' a Périgourdin once told me. His father probably drank it three times a day, for until recently soup was the breakfast drink as well, though this has almost universally been replaced now by coffee. And it is not thin consommé served in small quantities. Generally thickened with haricot beans or vermicelli, it is poured on to slices of bread at the bottom of the tureen—a custom known as 'tremper la soupe'. Once when watching a neighbour preparing lunch for several people who were helping her husband cut the maize, I exclaimed at the thickness of the soup which Madame was putting through the food mill and asked whether she was going to thin it down with stock, because it seemed to me that when mixed with the bread it would end up with a consistency of porridge. She replied that for her personal taste it would be too thick, but if she thinned it too much the men would not eat it, because to them soup had to be thick and satisfying or else it was not worth calling soup. Most of them take two helpings, leaving a spoonful or two when they have finished; this is then swilled round with a little wine, and the whole is drunk straight from the bowl without a spoon, a practice known as 'faire chabrol' and common all over south-west France.

People may ask themselves what is so special about the cookery of this part of south-western France, apart from its truffles and foie gras. In the preceding paragraphs and the following recipes, I have tried to show that there is much more to the cookery of this region than these. It is not generally to be found in the hotels on the ordinary menus, unless one is very lucky, but rather in the private homes and farmhouses, or in the tiny café restaurants in the villages, where over a glass of wine or some other aperitif the meal is discussed and ordered a day in advance. To those—and there are now quite a few—who like myself own houses in the area, the cooking in such restaurants needs no introduction. For others, with only two or three weeks' holiday, pressing on southwards to the sun and the sea in the south of France or Spain, there is often no time to stay and search out

Le chabrol: *the dregs of the soup mixed with wine*

such places. It is, however, not only for those who may have tasted some of the better-known specialities on their journeys that I have written this book, but to make available to a wider public some of the lesser-known recipes. Some of them may seem strange at first, but one should remember that they were evolved out of the local ingredients to hand at a time when there was no suitable means of distribution from one part of the country to another, no canning or deep-freezing. If on reading this book people are encouraged to try out some of these dishes in their

20

own kitchens, and thereby capture some of the atmosphere and flavour of this lovely part of France, so noted for its fine cooking, then I shall have succeeded in passing on some of the pleasure I have had in collecting the recipes.

Because life and so much of the cooking in the Périgord and the Quercy are geared to the seasons, I have deliberately followed that sequence in this book. Many local recipes have had to be omitted for lack of space. Some of those included have had to be adapted for kitchens outside France. I have tried to cut down on the number of dishes where truffles and foie gras are essential elements, although I cannot leave them out altogether. Many of these dishes are fast disappearing in the region itself due to the expense of the ingredients and their increasing export to Paris and abroad. Nevertheless, most of the other ingredients and flavourings mentioned in the recipes are obtainable outside France. More and more people living in the country or with cottages there are growing their own fruit, herbs and vegetables, and in towns herbs are grown increasingly in pots on window ledges. Unfamiliar mushrooms such as *cèpes* and *chanterelles*, although difficult to obtain from any but the most enterprising greengrocers, grow in woods and dried ones are available from most good delicatessen shops and can be substituted for the fresh ones in soups and stews etc.

Regarding spices and flavourings, all of those mentioned except perhaps *quatre épices* are obtainable. Much used in the cookery of south-west France, this is a combination of ground spices consisting of white peppercorns or allspice, nutmeg, cloves and cinnamon, usually in the proportions of 6 parts pepper or allspice to 1 part of each of the other spices, although it can be varied to suit your taste. It is easily made at home with the electric grinder.

Aniseed grains are obtainable from Oriental grocery stores, but some people prefer to use aniseed water to flavour puddings. This can be made at home by pouring boiling water on to a handful of the grains and leaving them to infuse for 20 minutes before straining. If this is not strong enough for your taste, try adding a few drops of Marie Brizard aniseed liqueur or Pernod.

For mustard, the true French Dijon mustard should be used; *Grey Poupon* or *Maille* are the brands most easily obtainable. If you are in France, most *charcuteries* and the Monoprix chain stores sell Dijon mustard in kilo and half-kilo jars, which work out much cheaper.

Walnut oil is not easy to obtain, but if you can get it, use it in salad dressings and other recipes in place of olive oil. It imparts a unique flavour to salads and sauces, such as the Roquefort sauce and mayonnaise. Because it is expensive and has a fairly strong taste, some cooks in the Périgord like to mix it with *Arachid* or ground-nut oil in equal proportions.

Vinegar. Use French red or white wine vinegar. Malt vinegar is far too strong and gives the wrong flavour to salad dressings and sauces. Most people in the Périgord make their own vinegar, starting it off with the sediment at the bottom of the wine barrels after they have drawn off the wine. This is obviously not possible here, but the strained 'heel' of a bottle of wine can be added to your vinegar if you are running short.

Wine. Where white wine is mentioned, unless otherwise specified use a fairly dry wine or dry white vermouth, which gives a highly aromatic flavour to *court bouillons* for fish and is excellent when a few drops are poured over fish to be grilled or wrapped in foil or baked. For red wine, the housewife in the Périgord or the Quercy would probably use a local Bergerac or Cahors wine or one from the neighbouring Médoc. The first two are not easy to obtain, so wherever possible use a carafe Bordeaux, of which there are several inexpensive brands on the market.

Brandy. None of the recipes in this book calls for the finest old cognac. Therefore use the pure French Grape Brandy, which is cheaper than most brands and on sale at most wine stores.

Chapter Two

SPRING AND SUMMER

SPRING comes in a sudden rush to the departments south of
the Loire. After the March rains and the cold spells—called
Gitoulés de Mars—the days lengthen, the air is warmer, though
the nights are still cool, and the wind no longer howls round
the farmhouses on the hills and plateaux with such force as
in the winter. Where before, the countryside has presented a
sad aspect, with brown bare ploughed fields, leafless trees and
woods, all changes within almost a matter of days. The grass
and crops begin to shoot up, the trees bud with fresh green
leaves and the meadows and hedgerows are thick with cowslips,
called *coucou* locally because they flower at the same time as
the first cuckoos are heard. On the houses and in the vineyards
the vines, pruned back severely in March and early April, begin
sprouting tiny leaves and minute bunches of grapes, no bigger
than a fingernail. The cuttings from the vines are tied into
bundles, laid out and left to dry in the sun for three or four
months before being burnt on the large open fires, to make the

embers on which meat and fish are grilled or roasted on revolving spits.

Towards the middle of April and May the young green corn, barley and oats contrast with the brilliant yellow of the mustard and calza fields—the last crop used as a component in certain types of fuel and motor oils—and the hedgerows and woods are filled with may, wild plum blossom and laburnum, which grows almost wild. In the old days, this last was used to separate different properties in the Périgord, instead of the more familiar wood and wire fencing seen nowadays. The gardens too suddenly burst out into colour, with yellow daffodils and white narcissi, tulips of all sizes and colours and, at the beginning of May, snowball trees and lilac, which grows in profusion. Ranging in tone from white to deepest mauve, great bunches of it fill vases in every household, scenting the air. Outside the houses stand pots filled with petunias, pansies and magnificent geraniums, which go on flowering throughout the summer. Not even the poorest houses, such as those on the stony *Causses* or plateaux in the south of the Périgord and in the Quercy, are without their pots of flowers.

In the vegetable gardens the plastic covers protecting the young lettuces, broad beans and other spring vegetables from the morning frosts are taken off, the first peas and beans are planted, and the young shoots of the garlic are cut and finely chopped and added to spring vegetable soups, stews and salads, or scattered as a garnish over ham and veal dishes, providing a more subtle flavour than a whole clove. Everybody is out in the fields or in the gardens, planting, weeding and fertilising the crops. This last is very necessary, for although the Périgord (and more particularly the Dordogne) was called 'the generous earth' by the British author Philip Oyler who lived there, it is only by constant hard work that the province can be made to yield so much. In many parts of the province the soil is thin and poor and the limestone, which forms such magnificent

24

grottoes and caves as those at Lascaux, Les Eyzies and Rouffig-
nac, needs to be constantly broken up, heavily manured and
fertilised. The same is true further south and to the east in the
province of the Quercy, where on the plateaux forming such
a large proportion of the country all that can be raised are sheep.
Once one gets away from the fertile valleys of the Lot and the
Dordogne, life is a constant battle against the forces of nature.
In the spring the wind coming from the north and the east is
dreaded, for it has a drying quality, turning to yellow the young
crops and shrivelling them up. In the summer, too, the stranger
who thinks that the west wind will bring relief from the heat
is soon disillusioned. This wind is hot and may go on for days,
only to be followed by one of those spectacular thunderstorms
with forks of electric lightning, torrential rain or large hail-
stones which damage the young vines and fruit trees and beat
down the corn and maize fields, ruining the harvests.

The markets in April and May are a beautiful sight: the
vegetable stalls piled high with tight fluffy cauliflowers, bunches
of young leeks and carrots, little new potatoes and the first of
the broad beans, so young and tender that they can be eaten raw
with salt as part of the hors d'oeuvres. Later in the season they
will be made into soups, purées and ragouts with little onions
and eaten with cooked hams or salt pork. Usually as one wanders
round the market one comes across peasant women displaying
freshly picked asparagus, lettuces and mushrooms, bunches of
chives and parsley and occasionally homemade goat or sheep
milk cheeses. These women are worth seeking out, for their
produce is often fresher and cheaper than that on the stalls. On
the fish stalls, the silvery mackerel and sardines lie neatly piled
up next to the mounds of small pink crawfish and crabs, whilst
the lampreys and eels squirm live in their boxes, ready to be
killed and cooked in wine with pieces of fat salt pork, shallots
and garlic, the sauce carefully bound with their blood, or to be
grilled and then served with a hard-boiled egg and herb sauce.

Most beautiful at this time of the year are the flower and plant stalls, a riot of colour with their geraniums, petunias and pansies, red and white begonias, young stocks, orange and lemon marigolds, hydrangeas, primulas and sweet williams. It is difficult not to lose one's head and buy indiscriminately.

Soon, however, this sudden rush of spring with its burst of flowers and blossom will change: the *grosses chaleurs*, fierce heats of the summer, generally begin in June, and in July the temperature often rises to 90°F—32°C and over. The earth becomes as hard as the rock it covers and the water in the wells sinks to dangerously low levels. To protect themselves from the sun, the women wear white or blue linen bonnets called *quichenottes* with long pleated frills covering the backs of their necks. Roses, peonies, dahlias, gladioli and golden rod replace the daffodils and tulips in the gardens, whilst on the houses, wistaria and climbing roses cover the walls and eaves.

For the housewife, if she is not in the fields helping her husband, this is the second great season of the year when the steriliser comes into its own. Beans, peas and other young vegetables are bottled and stored away for the winter, together with the cherries and plums. The blackcurrants are almost universally made into liqueurs and the peach trees, before the fruit is ripe, are stripped of some of their leaves, which are then macerated in sugar, wine and spirit, the resulting liquid drunk as an aperitif. Tradition has it that this and the wine made from the leaves of walnut trees should be made on Midsummer Eve; if these drinks are made a day or so later, so the superstition runs, the alcohol will over-ferment and 'dance' in the bottle and bad luck will fall on the house.

For the farmers, the summer months from July to the end of September are some of the busiest of the year, with the haymaking and harvesting of the crops. The tractors are taken out before dawn and in many cases work continues until after nightfall, the headlights on the tractors lightings the fields in the dark.

26

Most of the farmers are freeholders, farming an average of 35 acres, and consequently farm labourers employed by the proprietors are rarely seen, since all the work is done by the family itself. Most villages, however, have their own communal combine harvester, which the mayor lets out to individuals as and when it is needed.

And so, throughout the hot summer, whilst the tourists flock in their thousands to visit the painted caves and castles, life for the farming families is one of intense activity. Perhaps in a few years' time, if there is enough money saved and all has gone well, the farm can be handed over to the son who has remained working on the land, and the farmer and his wife can then take a holiday.

SOUPS

LA FRICASSEE and LE FARCI
Fricassée and Stuffing

The basis of soups in the south-west of France is the *fricassée*. Either the vegetables which go into the soup are fried gently and sprinkled with flour to make a roux before the liquid is added, or a few of them are taken out about half an hour before the soup is to be served, fried with a little fresh celery or leek, garlic, parsley, a few rounds of turnip or carrot, and perhaps bacon, and then put back into the soup to simmer for another 15 minutes or so. There is no hard and fast rule about the exact ingredients, or whether the vegetables are fried first or later. It is a question of individual taste, some cooks swearing by the first method, others by the second. What they are all agreed on is that without the *fricassée* the soup would not have enough body and flavour.

The *farci* is a mixture of breadcrumbs soaked in a little milk

27

or stock, garlic, onion, parsley and meat, the whole bound with eggs and then wrapped up in cabbage leaves, which is then put to cook in the soup. The meat can be ham, cold chicken, beef or pork—whatever happens to be on hand. When the soup is to be served, the *farci* is taken out and cut into slices by the husband or male head of the family, who distributes it round the table. The saying *Qu'ey pas éou qué copo lou farchi* is still heard in many Périgourdine villages, signifying a hen-pecked husband whose wife is the real authority in the home and therefore cuts the *farci*.

This is one version:

6 oz minced gammon or fresh pork
3 oz unsmoked streaky bacon
1 small onion
2 cloves garlic
2 eggs
6 oz fresh white breadcrumbs
1 tablespoonful parsley
4 cabbage leaves
a little milk or stock from the soup

Serves 4 to 6

Soak the breadcrumbs in the milk or stock and then squeeze out the liquid with your hands. Chop together the onion, garlic and parsley and add to the breadcrumbs along with the gammon or pork and the finely chopped bacon. Season with pepper and a very little salt and bind with the eggs. Pour boiling water over the cabbage leaves and leave them for 5 minutes. Drain them and wrap up the *farci* in them. Tie round with string or strong cotton and simmer in the soup for 30 minutes.

LE MOUTAIROL
Saffron Soup

In the old days saffron was grown extensively in the Lot and commonly used as a flavouring in soups, stews and other dishes. Now, as everywhere, it has become increasingly rare and many of the old recipes calling for it have died out. There were two versions of the Moutairol, for instance, the following soup and a casserole of minced beef with turnips and chestnuts, both of which were eaten at festivals and on holidays. I have seen references to the latter in several old books, but have never been able to find the actual recipe. The soup, made also in the neighbouring region of the Aveyron, has survived as a very simple peasant soup.

$2\frac{1}{2}$–3 pints well flavoured chicken stock
1 small loaf white bread
2 carrots
1 onion
1 turnip
2 leeks
2 packets saffron
   salt, pepper, a bouquet garni

Serves 4 to 6

Simmer the vegetables in the chicken stock with the bouquet garni until they are very tender. Slice the bread thinly and cut into small pieces. Add to the soup and simmer, stirring often, for 20 minutes. Put the whole soup through a sieve, add the saffron, correct the seasoning and simmer another 5 minutes.

29

LA SOUPE DE FEVES
Broad Bean Soup

3 lb broad beans
1 tablespoonful pork, duck or goose fat
1 tablespoonful flour
2 leeks
1 stick celery
6 very small white onions or spring onions
3 rashers unsmoked bacon blanched in water for
   5 minutes
1 sprig thyme
1 clove garlic
2 sprigs parsley

Serves 4 to 6

Shell the beans. Unless they are old and tough do not remove the inner skins. Melt the fat in the bottom of the pan and turn the sliced leeks, celery and onions in it until they are softened but not browned. Add the blanched and diced bacon and fry gently for 2 or 3 minutes. Sprinkle over the flour to make a roux and add 3 pints water. Add the beans, the garlic finely chopped and the herbs. Season with salt and pepper and simmer slowly for 1 hour.

LE TOURIN BLANCHI A L'OSEILLE
Sorrel Soup

$\frac{1}{4}$ lb sorrel leaves
2 potatoes
3 cloves garlic
1 egg, separated
1 tablespoonful butter, pork or goose fat

3 pints water
a few drops of vinegar
salt and pepper

Serves 4 to 6

Soften the sorrel with the chopped garlic and peeled and quartered potatoes in the fat for 10 minutes, watching carefully to see that they do not burn. Add the flour and then the water gradually. Season with salt and pepper and boil gently for 30 minutes. Take out the potatoes and mash them smooth. Put the purée back into the soup and add the egg white, stirring vigorously so that it separates into small pieces as it coagulates. Simmer for another 5 minutes, then bind the soup with the egg yolk beaten up with the vinegar. Do not let the soup boil after you have added the yolk.

LA SOUPE AU PERSIL PAYSANNE
Parsley Soup

2 large handfuls of parsley with their stalks
2 leeks

1 carrot, grated
1 clove garlic
1 heaped tablespoonful diced salt pork or bacon
2 tablespoonfuls butter, goose or pork fat
1 tablespoonful flour
2½ pints water or stock
   salt and pepper
   a sprig of thyme and a bayleaf

Serves 4 to 6

Chop together finely the white part of one of the leeks with the parsley and the garlic. Melt a tablespoonful of fat in a heavy saucepan and gently fry them in it until they have softened. Watch to see they do not burn. Sprinkle over the flour and when this has taken on a little colour, add the water or stock, thyme and bayleaf, salt and pepper. Simmer for 30 minutes. Melt the rest of the fat in a frying pan and fry the bacon, the other leek finely chopped and the grated carrot for about 5 minutes or until the bacon and leek are lightly browned. Add to the soup and continue simmering another 15 minutes.

SOUPE AUX HARICOTS ET TOMATES
Bean and Tomato Soup

1 lb haricot beans
1½ lb tomatoes
2 onions
3 cloves garlic
2 tablespoonfuls oil—walnut oil if possible
2 tablespoonfuls chopped parsley
   a sprig of thyme
1 bayleaf

32

3 pints water
salt and pepper

Serves 4 to 6

Soak the beans overnight. Peel and roughly chop the tomatoes.
Chop the onions and garlic and fry them gently in the oil with
the tomatoes for 10 minutes. They should soften almost to a
purée without taking on much colour. Add the beans, the thyme,
the bayleaf and the water. Season with salt and pepper, cover
and cook for 1½ hours. The soup should be very thick. Just
before serving, stir in the parsley.

EGGS

OEUFS A L'AGENAISE
Eggs Baked with Aubergines

4 aubergines
4 eggs
1 onion
1 clove garlic
1 dessertspoonful chopped parsley
1 oz butter
3 tablespoonfuls oil
salt and pepper

Serves 4

Peel the aubergines, cut them into slices (not too finely),
sprinkle them with salt and leave them to drain in a colander
with a plate on top for 1 hour. Wipe them carefully and fry
them gently in the butter and oil, seasoned with the pepper
until they are tender. Remove with a slotted spoon to an oval

c   33

fireproof dish. Chop the onion and garlic very finely and add to the fat in the pan; if the aubergines have absorbed all the fat, add a little more oil. Soften the onion and garlic without letting them burn—they should be a pale gold in colour—and then mix in the parsley. Break the eggs on top of the aubergines and scatter the onion and parsley mixture over the top. Season lightly with salt and pepper and bake in the oven, Gas 4—355°F, until the eggs are set.

OEUFS POCHES A LA TOMATE
Eggs Poached in Tomato Sauce

1 pint fresh tomato sauce
1 egg per person
2 tablespoonfuls chopped parsley
2 cloves garlic finely chopped
1 very thin slice cooked ham

Heat the tomato sauce gently and stir in the parsley, garlic and ham. Then very carefully poach the eggs in the sauce one by one. Keep them warm whilst you are poaching the other eggs. Pour the tomato sauce over them and serve surrounded by triangles of fried bread.

OMELETTE AUX ASPERGES
Asparagus Omelette

This is not the normal asparagus omelette in which the asparagus, boiled until just tender and then turned in butter, is mixed in with the beaten eggs or put in the centre after the omelette has been made.

a ragout d'asperges (see page 39)
5 eggs

34

1 slice white bread weighing about 1½oz
1½ oz butter
   salt and pepper

Serves 4

Cut the bread into small squares and fry in the butter until golden. Beat up the eggs, season with salt and pepper and pour over the bread. Give the mixture a quick stir and make the omelette in the usual way. Turn it out flat on to a dish and pour the asparagus over it.

OMELETTE AUX CEPES SECS
Dried Mushroom Omelette

1 oz dried mushrooms
6 eggs
1 tablespoonful chopped parsley
2 cloves garlic
2 tablespoonfuls oil

Serves 4

Soak the mushrooms for 10 minutes in hot water, then rinse under a running tap to get rid of any dust and grit and dry them on a cloth. Heat the oil in the pan and fry the mushrooms, chopped garlic and parsley together for 10 minutes. Beat up the eggs in a bowl, season with salt and pepper and add to the mushrooms. Stir quickly to mix the eggs and mushrooms for a minute, and then make the omelette in the usual way. See that the pan in which you make this omelette is large enough—it must be at least 12 inches in diameter if you wish to make one for 4 people.

OMELETTE AUX CROUTONS ET OSEILLE
Sorrel and Crouton Omelette

6 eggs
1 slice of white bread cut into cubes
a large handful of sorrel
1 tablespoonful thin cream
1 oz butter
salt and pepper

Serves 4

Wash the sorrel and tear it into strips. Melt the butter in a large omelette pan and fry the bread until it is soft and golden. Add the sorrel and let this melt with the bread for a couple of minutes. Beat up the eggs with the cream and season with salt and pepper. Add to the pan, stir quickly to mix and make the omelette in the normal way. Rub the top of the omelette with a nut of butter before serving.

This is one of the most typical omelettes eaten in the Périgord.

FLAN AUX COURGETTES
Courgettes Baked with Eggs and Cheese

A flan in France does not automatically mean the same as in Britain or the United States, where a flan is more often than not a sweet, with fruit on a sponge or pastry base. In France, a flan generally means a mixture of eggs and milk beaten together and baked in the oven. Various ingredients can be added to make an hors d'oeuvres or separate vegetable dish, or sugar can be added and it is served at the end of the meal, becoming what is known to us as baked custard. This recipe, which comes from the Quercy, makes a very good hors d'oeuvres or vegetable dish.

36

1 lb courgettes or baby squash
2 oz grated cheese
4 eggs
½ pint milk
  salt and pepper

Serves 4

Unless they are very large or are ridgy, do not peel the cour-gettes. Wash and slice them on the bias, sprinkle with salt and leave to drain for 1 hour in a colander with a weighted plate on top. Rinse them and blanch in very slightly salted water for 5 minutes. Drain thoroughly on a cloth and put them into an ovenproof dish. Cover with the grated cheese. Beat the eggs and the milk together, season with salt and pepper and pour over the courgettes. Bake in a hot oven, Gas 6—400°F, for 35 minutes, by which time the eggs will have set and the dish will be puffed and golden.

A little diced ham can be added to make the dish more sub-stantial.

CROQUETTES D'OEUFS AUX CHAMPIGNONS ET JAMBON
Egg Croquettes with Mushrooms and Ham

4 hard-boiled eggs
½ pint thick bechamel or white sauce
2 oz sliced mushrooms
2 oz diced ham
1 onion, finely chopped
1 dessertspoonful chopped parsley
2 cloves garlic, finely chopped
1 oz butter
1 egg white

37

breadcrumbs
oil or lard for frying

Serves 4 to 6

Fry the onion and mushrooms in the butter until soft and add to the bechamel, together with the parsley, garlic and ham. Chop the eggs finely and add to the mixture. Season with salt and pepper. Spread out on a plate or large dish and chill till next day. Flour your hands and form the mixture into little croquettes or flat round cakes. Dip in the beaten egg white and then roll in the breadcrumbs. Fry in the oil or lard until golden all over.

VEGETABLES

FONDS D'ARTICHAUTS 'RECAMIER'
Stuffed Baked Artichoke Hearts

Allow 1 large artichoke heart per person.
    6 artichoke hearts
    4 oz mousse or crème de foie
    1 oz gruyère cheese
    ½ pint fairly thick creamy bechamel sauce
    2 oz butter

Serves 6

Boil the artichokes till tender in salted water, pull off all the leaves and the choke and trim the artichokes' hearts. Fry them for 1 minute on each side in the butter. Drain. Put a layer of the mousse or crème de foie on each heart and place in a shallow fireproof dish. Cover with the bechamel and grate the cheese over the top. Put into a hot oven, Gas 7—425°F, for 5 minutes.

LE RAGOUT D'ASPERGES
Asparagus Stew

1½ lb asparagus
6 silverskin or pickling onions
1 pint vegetable or chicken stock
1 clove garlic
1 tablespoonful chopped parsley
1 dessertspoonful flour
1 oz butter
1 sugar lump

Serves 4

Scrape the asparagus, wash and cut into 1½ inch lengths. Melt the butter and fry the onions and garlic until they are golden. Sprinkle over the flour and add the stock, the asparagus, the parsley and the sugar lump. Season with salt and pepper and simmer very gently for 35 to 40 minutes. Good with cold meat or chicken. Sometimes ½lb of petits pois are added at the same time as the asparagus to the ragout.

RAGOUT DE FEVES
Broad Beans Stewed with Onions and Celery

3 lb broad beans
12 small pickling onions or round spring onions
1 small celery heart
1 oz pure pork lard, goose or duck fat
1 clove garlic
1 cup vegetable, chicken or veal stock
1 dessertspoonful flour
  a sprig of thyme, parsley and rosemary
½ oz butter

Serves 4

Shell the beans, peel the onions and halve the celery heart. Turn the onions in the fat for a few minutes but do not let them brown. Sprinkle the flour over them, stirring well, and simmer for a minute until pale golden in colour. Add the beans, celery, herbs and garlic and then the stock, stirring to avoid lumps. Season with salt and pepper, cover the pan and simmer very gently for 20 minutes or until the beans are cooked and tender. Extract the rosemary (throw it away) and a ladleful of the beans. Sieve these and add the butter to the purée. Return to the pan and cook uncovered for another 5 minutes.

HARICOTS VERTS QUERCYNOISE
French Beans in Egg Sauce

1 lb green beans
2 eggs
1 tablespoonful vinegar
1 clove garlic

40

2 shallots
salt and pepper

Serves 4

Boil the beans in salted water until just tender. Drain, reserving 1 tablespoonful of the liquid. Beat this in a bowl together with the eggs and the vinegar. Pour over the beans, add the very finely chopped shallots and garlic and stir over a very low flame until the beans are covered in a thick creamy sauce. Serve with a little chopped parsley scattered over.

LES HARICOTS A LA COUENNE
Haricot Beans with Salt Pork

Haricot beans are cultivated in every vegetable garden in the Périgord and the Quercy, and this way of cooking them is one of the most common. They are generally cooked with the pork rind which has been cut into strips, rolled up and preserved with the confit of pork, but towards May or June most of this has been used up, and fresh pork rind and salt pork bought from the butcher or *charcutier* is substituted.

1 lb haricot beans
$\frac{1}{4}$ lb salt pork
6 oz fresh pork rind
3 tomatoes
1 onion stuck with a clove
2 cloves garlic
2 tablespoonfuls chopped parsley
thyme and a bayleaf

Serves 4 to 6

41

Soak the beans overnight. Drain them and put in a pan covered with fresh water. Boil gently for 1 hour together with the onion and the pork rind, previously blanched in salted water for 5 minutes, salt, pepper, thyme and the bayleaf. Meanwhile dice the salt pork and let it brown in its own fat in a pan. Add the crushed garlic and the chopped tomatoes and parsley and fry gently for 5 minutes. Add to the beans and continue cooking gently for a further 1½ hours, or until the beans are very tender. They should be creamy, having absorbed most of the liquid, but still whole.

FONDUE A L'OSEILLE
Sorrel Purée

Sorrel is very easily cultivated as well as growing wild in fields. It is eaten in the spring when the leaves are young and tender and not yet too acid, after which it is cut and given to the rabbits during the summer.

2 lb sorrel
1 egg yolk
1 oz flour
1 oz butter
½ pint milk or vegetable stock

Serves 4

Boil the sorrel in slightly salted water for 3 minutes. Drain thoroughly. Melt the fat in an enamel or fireproof porcelain saucepan and turn the sorrel in it for 10 minutes, stirring with a wooden spoon to prevent it catching on the bottom. Sprinkle the flour over it and gradually add the warmed milk or stock. Season with pepper and salt, and simmer for 10 minutes. Beat up the egg yolk with a few drops of water and bind the purée with it. The purée is generally eaten with a piece of preserved goose or duck or the stuffed neck, but is also good with poached or fried eggs and ham.

CROQUETTES DE POMMES DE TERRE AUX NOIX
Potato and Walnut Croquettes

> 1 lb potatoes
> 3 oz walnuts
> 2 cloves garlic
>   oil for frying
> 1 tablespoonful chopped parsley
> 1 oz melted butter
> 2 eggs
> 1 extra egg white

> *Serves 4 to 6*

Steam the potatoes and mash them. Chop the nuts very finely and add to the potatoes, with the parsley and crushed garlic. Add the melted butter and the two egg yolks. Mix well together and season highly with salt and black pepper. Fold in the stiffly beaten egg whites, flour your hands lightly, and form the mixture into little croquettes. Beat the extra egg white until it is frothy, dip the croquettes into it and deep fry in boiling hot oil until they are a rich golden brown. Serve round a roast, or with tomato sauce and a salad.

GRATIN DE POTIRON ET TOMATES
Baked Pumpkin and Tomatoes

> 1 lb tomatoes
> 2 lb pumpkin—weight when peeled
> 2 cloves garlic
> 2 tablespoonfuls chopped parsley

43

1½ oz breadcrumbs
6 tablespoonfuls oil
½ oz butter

Serves 4

Cut the pumpkin into slices about ½ inch thick and 3 inches long. Blanch them for 5 minutes in salted water and then drain them thoroughly on a cloth. Melt half the oil in a frying pan and fry them gently until they begin to look transparent. Put them into a shallow ovenproof dish. Add the rest of the oil and fry the sliced tomatoes in this, together with the crushed garlic and half the parsley. Season with salt and pepper. When the tomatoes begin to form a purée and some of the moisture has dried up, put them on top of the pumpkin. Mix the rest of the parsley with the breadcrumbs and cover the tomatoes. Dot with the butter and bake for 20 minutes in a moderately hot oven, Gas 6 —400°F.

RAGOUT DE LEGUMES PERIGOURDIN
Périgourdine Vegetable Stew

1 lb potatoes
1 lb tomatoes
2 large onions
2 oz duck, pork or goose fat
1 tablespoonful juniper berries
3 tablespoonfuls meat stock
   salt and pepper

Serves 4

Peel the onions and potatoes and cut into thin rounds. Cut the tomatoes into thin slices also. Grease a fireproof dish with some of the fat and put in a layer of potatoes. Add a layer of onions and then tomatoes. Dot with some of the fat, scatter over half the juniper berries and season with salt and pepper. Repeat the layers, dotting here and there with the fat and scattering over the rest of the juniper berries, but finish with a layer of potatoes. Season again with salt and pepper and add the meat stock. Cover with foil or the lid of the dish and bake in a moderately hot oven, Gas 5—375°F, for 50 minutes to 1 hour, by which time the vegetables should be tender.

FISH

ANGUILLES AUX PRUNEAUX
Eels with Prunes

1 large eel or 2 medium eels
1½ lb leeks
½ lb stoned prunes
5 tablespoonfuls oil
¼ pint red wine
¼ pint water

Serves 4

Skin and clean the fish and cut into thick slices. Fry them in the oil until they are half cooked. Remove and keep warm. Add the cleaned and sliced leeks to the oil in the pan and the wine and water. Cover and cook until the leeks are very tender. Put through a sieve. Put the fish, the sieved leeks and the prunes into a clean pan, season with salt and pepper and simmer 15 minutes.

In the Périgord and the Quercy this dish is more often cooked with lampreys but since these are practically impossible to obtain in Britain and the United States, I have substituted eels.

LA BLANQUETTE D'ANGUILLE
Stewed Eels in White Wine

2 large eels
4 cloves garlic, 12 very small onions
2 tablespoonfuls parsley
2 egg yolks
1 dessertspoonful vinegar
1 tablespoonful flour
1 pint water
$\frac{3}{4}$ pint white wine
$\frac{1}{2}$ pint oil

Serves 4 to 6

Cover the bottom of a heavy pan with half the oil and slowly fry the eels, skinned and cut into large slices, until they are golden all over. Remove with a slotted spoon to a dish and keep warm. Throw away the oil, rinse out the pan and pour in the rest of the oil. Turn the onions, garlic and parsley in the fresh oil until they are softened, sprinkle over the flour and add the wine and water. Put back the eel slices, season with salt and pepper and cook very slowly for 25 minutes, at the end of which time they should be cooked through and tender. Beat up the yolks with the vinegar and thicken the sauce with the liaison. *Do not boil* once you have added the egg yolks.

46

COURT BOUILLON DE POISSON A LA MODE DE PERIGORD
Périgourdine Fish Bouillon

(For Brill, Carp, Pike, Perch and Tench)

5 cloves garlic
   a handful of parsley
1 pint white wine
2 oz butter
2 oz flour
   salt and pepper

Quantities sufficient for a 2½lb fish

Crush the garlic in a mortar with the parsley, add the white wine and season with salt and pepper. Pour over the fish. Make a roux with the butter and flour in a pan, moisten with a ladleful of the liquid and add to the fish. Poach for 45 minutes or 1 hour, according to the size of the fish. Every ten minutes, syphon off some of the court bouillon to the pan in which the roux was made, bring to the boil and return to the fish. Serve in a deep dish, with the sauce poured over, and accompany with pieces of toast rubbed over on both sides with a cut clove of garlic.

MAQUERAUX AUX ASPERGES
Mackerel and Asparagus Salad

3 mackerel
3 medium sized potatoes
1 clove garlic
4 tablespoonfuls olive oil
2 tablespoonfuls of vinegar or lemon juice
1 heaped teaspoonful French mustard

47

1 pinch nutmeg
1 pinch of thyme
1 dessertspoonful chopped parsley
1 dessertspoonful chopped chives
1 sprig chervil
1 egg yolk
1 lb thin green asparagus
court bouillon as described on page 200

Serves 4

Simmer all the ingredients for the court bouillon together for 20 minutes and then poach the cleaned mackerel in the liquid. When they are cooked and are cool enough to handle, skin and bone them, break them up into pieces and put them into a bowl together with the potatoes boiled in their skins and then mashed. Mash well with a fork and add the vinegar or lemon juice, the oil, mustard, nutmeg, herbs, finely chopped garlic and salt and pepper to taste. Finally mix in the egg yolk. Mix well and chill. Serve on a flat dish with the asparagus, boiled until tender and dressed with a little oil and lemon juice, arranged all around. In the winter this is served garnished with hard-boiled eggs instead of asparagus.

MAQUEREAUX AUX VERJUS
Mackerel with Green Grapes

Allow 1 large mackerel weighing at least $1\frac{1}{2}$lb for every two people.

2 mackerel
$1\frac{1}{2}$ lb slightly under-ripe green grapes
$\frac{1}{2}$ pint dry white wine
2 onions
2 carrots

2 sprigs fennel—dried or fresh
1 oz butter
salt and pepper

Serves 4

Clean the fish, rub the insides with salt and pepper and place
a sprig of fennel inside each fish. Peel the onions and carrots and
slice very thinly. Put the vegetables in the bottom of an ovenproof dish large enough to hold the fish comfortably, place the
mackerel on top and pour over the white wine. Bake in a moderate oven, Gas 4—355°F, for 35 minutes. Press half the grapes
through a sieve to extract the juice and add this to the fish halfway through the cooking. Baste often with the juices. Peel and
pip the rest of the grapes and fry them in the butter for 5 minutes. Remove the fish to a serving dish and surround with the
grapes. Cover and keep warm. Strain the juices from the ovenproof dish into the butter, stir well and boil down hard for 5
minutes. Correct the seasoning and pour over the fish. Serve
with steamed or boiled new potatoes.

LES TRUITES MARINEES
Marinated Trout

For 4 trout:
4 sprigs thyme
2 lemons
4 fluid oz olive or arachid oil
4 fluid oz fish stock made from fish bones
   and trimmings or a cod's head, an onion
   stuck with a clove, a bouquet garni and
   water, salt and pepper
½ pint white wine

D
49

a bouquet garni
a pinch of quatre épices or nutmeg
6 peppercorns
2 finely chopped shallots or 2 tablespoonfuls
chopped spring onions
2 hard-boiled eggs
2 oz blanched almonds

Serves 4

Add the oil, wine, peppercorns and spice, bouquet garni and salt to the fish stock. Simmer for 40 minutes. Put a lemon slice and a sprig of thyme into the cavity of each trout and wrap them in oiled foil. Bake in a moderate oven, Gas 4—355°F, for 30 minutes. Unwrap and skin the fish as soon as they are cool enough to handle. Put them into a long, fairly deep serving dish, and scatter over the shallots or spring onions. Bring the oil and

wine mixture to the boil and boil fast for 5 minutes. Strain over the fish. Chill, turning the trout occasionally. Garnish with the almonds, cut into slivers and slices of hard-boiled eggs. Just before serving, squeeze the juice of the other lemon over it.

TRUITE FARCIE AU CONFIT
Trout Stuffed with Preserved Duck

I would not suggest opening a tin or jar of confit specially for this dish, but if you have some preserved duck left over from another meal and there is not enough to go round, this is an unusual way of using it up. If you have enough to give six or seven tablespoonfuls when chopped, you will need in addition to this and 4 trout:

1 medium sized onion
1 clove garlic
1 lemon
1 tablespoonful chopped parsley
2 tablespoonfuls breadcrumbs
   salt and pepper
   aluminium foil
   fat from the bottom of the confit jar or tin

Serves 4

Fry the chopped onion and garlic in a dessertspoonful of the fat from the preserved duck until they have softened. Add the parsley and finely chopped meat and fry gently for a further minute. Mix in the breadcrumbs and season with salt and pepper. Clean the trout, pat dry inside and out with kitchen paper or a clean cloth and stuff them with the mixture. Sew them up so that the stuffing cannot escape. Cut four large pieces of foil, large enough to enclose the fish, smear them generously with

some more of the fat, or, if there is not enough, oil them. Lay
the fish on them, moisten with a few drops of lemon juice and
then draw up the edges of the foil together so that the fish is
completely enclosed, twisting the ends carefully. Bake in the
oven, Gas 5—375°F, for 35 minutes.

A more everyday version is to replace the confit with the same
amount of fresh minced pork or mild gammon. The trout is then
either cooked in foil as above or baked, Gas 4—355°F, for 30
minutes, on a bed of finely sliced onions with a third of a pint
of white wine or fish stock poured over, the strained sauce being
bound at the last moment with the beaten yolk of an egg.

TRUITE EN CIVET QUERCYNOISE
Trout in Red Wine with Tarragon

4 trout
½ lb mushrooms
2 shallots
2 tablespoonfuls breadcrumbs
2 onions
2 carrots
3 rashers fat bacon
2 oz butter
1 bottle of Burgundy or Cahors
4 sprigs fresh tarragon or a large pinch of
   dried tarragon
2 sprigs each of thyme and parsley
2 crushed bayleaves
   a large pinch each of nutmeg and cinnamon
   beurre manié made with a heaped tablespoon
   each of flour and butter

Serves 4

Fry the very finely chopped mushrooms and shallots in the butter until they are softened. Add the breadcrumbs and chopped tarragon leaves. Season with salt and pepper and stuff the trout. Fasten with toothpicks. Put the fish on top of the sliced onions and carrots and diced bacon. Add the tarragon stalks and the rest of the herbs and spices, and pour over the wine. Cover with a piece of buttered paper and bake in a moderate oven, Gas 4—355°F, for 35 minutes, basting frequently. Remove the fish to a serving dish and keep warm. Strain the sauce and reduce by fast boiling. Thicken with the beurre manié, taste for seasoning and pour over the fish.

RAGOUT DE MORUE AUX CHAMPIGNONS
Salt Cod with Mushrooms

$1\frac{1}{2}$ lb salt cod
$\frac{1}{2}$ lb new potatoes
3 carrots
$\frac{1}{2}$ lb mushrooms
2 onions
$\frac{1}{4}$ lb fat unsmoked bacon
$\frac{1}{2}$ teacup olive oil
2 cloves garlic
1 bayleaf

Serves 4

Soak the cod overnight. Drain, cover with cold water and bring to the boil. Remove the pan from the fire and leave for 10 minutes. In separate pans half cook the potatoes and the carrots diced. Slice the onions, clean and slice the mushrooms and dice the bacon. Heat the oil and cook the potatoes, carrots and onions. When these are golden and softened add the bacon and cook

again gently until this is golden. Finally add the skinned and
boned cod, cut into small pieces, and the chopped garlic. Season
with freshly ground black pepper, a very little salt if necessary
and the bayleaf.

Cover the pan, leaving the lid tilted slightly so that the steam
can escape, and continue cooking gently for 10 minutes. Serve
with a little chopped parsley and, if liked, a squeeze of lemon
juice sprinkled over.

SNAILS

Tinned snails, ready for stuffing, are sold with their shells
packed separately in many delicatessens and at food departments
of the larger stores, thus dispensing with the tedious business of
starving, boiling, cleaning and rinsing. The country people in
France will tell you, however, that it is only the snails which
they themselves have gathered after the spring showers that are
worth the trouble of cooking and eating. The farmers in the
south-west say you must wait until well after dark—at least until
after 9.30pm—before a sufficient number of snails appear in the
grass and amongst the vines and can be gathered. Then, armed
with a torch and a large basket, whole families will go out look-
ing for them. Once collected they are put into boxes or pails, the
tops of which are covered with a fine wire mesh, to prevent them
from escaping, and starved for a fortnight to three weeks before
being boiled in wood ash and water.

ESCARGOTS AU VIN ROUGE
Snails in Red Wine

4 dozen snails
¼ lb unsmoked streaky bacon or mild gammon
2 oz breadcrumbs
3 cloves garlic

54

2 tablespoonfuls chopped parsley
1 egg
   a court bouillon (see page 200)

Sauce

¾ pint red wine
1 oz flour
2 oz butter
½ teaspoonful each cinnamon and quatre épices
1 lump sugar
1 sprig thyme
1 sprig parsley

Make a roux with the flour and half the butter, add the red wine, having previously set it alight in a small pan, stir till smooth and add the herbs and the spices. Season with salt and pepper and put to cook very slowly with an asbestos mat under the pan. Make a court bouillon (see page 200), bring to the boil, lower the heat and simmer for 20 minutes.

Chop or mince the bacon or gammon finely, crush the garlic and mix in a bowl together with the breadcrumbs, parsley and egg. Season with salt and pepper, taking into account the saltiness of the bacon or gammon.

If you are using tinned snails, add them to a court bouillon (see page 200) and simmer for 5 minutes. Fresh snails need 20 minutes' simmering. Drain them, but reserve the liquor. Stuff the shells with the snails and the stuffing and place them in an ovenproof dish, stuffed side up if possible. Taste the red wine sauce for seasoning; if it is too harsh add the sugar lump. Add the rest of the butter and, if it is too thick, thin down with a little of the reserved court bouillon. Pour it over the snails and heat up in a moderate oven for 5 to 10 minutes, basting every so often.

ESCARGOTS EN FRICASSEE DE POULET
Snails with White Wine and Mushrooms

The French name is the old-fashioned one for this dish, in spite of the fact that the recipe has nothing to do with chicken.

4 dozen snails
a court bouillon (see page 200)
½ lb button mushrooms
3 oz unsmoked streaky bacon
2 cloves garlic
2 tablespoonfuls chopped parsley
1 tablespoonful chopped chives
a sprig of thyme
1 bayleaf
2 egg yolks
1 oz butter
1 tablespoonful flour
a large pinch of nutmeg
a few drops of vinegar or lemon juice

Make a court bouillon (see page 200) and simmer the snails in it for 5 minutes. Melt the butter in a pan and sauté the diced bacon and the chopped mushrooms gently for 5 minutes. Add the crushed garlic and the drained snails, sprinkle over the flour and gradually add 1 pint of the reserved court bouillon liquid. Add the herbs, season with salt and pepper and simmer very gently for 15 minutes. Beat up the yolks with the vinegar or lemon juice and the nutmeg, pour into the pan and thicken the sauce with the liaison. *Do not let the mixture boil,* but serve very hot.

MEAT

LA DAUBE DE PRINTEMPS
Spring Beef Stew

Commonly eaten all over the south and south-west of France, this dish has, nevertheless, regional variations. Here is one which I was given by the proprietress of the Auberge du Moulin at St Martin de Redon, a little village not far from Puy l'Evêque in the Lot.

2 lb beef cut into large cubes
$\frac{1}{4}$ lb fresh pork rinds cut into strips
2 large onions
3 cloves garlic
1 lb new carrots
1 lb new potatoes
$\frac{1}{2}$ pint dry white wine
1 oz flour
   a bouquet garni of a sprig of thyme
   and rosemary, parsley and a bayleaf
1 pinch quatre épices
1 oz pork, duck or goose fat—*not* oil
   a persillade mixture of 2 tablespoonfuls
   chopped parsley, a small slice of lean ham
   and 2 cloves of garlic chopped together
   with the parsley
   salt and pepper

Serves 4 to 6

Fry the meats in a heavy cocotte in the melted fat until they are browned, add the sliced onions and the chopped garlic and fry them until they are golden. Sprinkle the flour over them, mix well and then add the white wine, the bouquet garni and the spice, salt and pepper. Cover and cook on top of an asbestos mat on the stove very gently for 1 hour. Then add the carrots. If you are using small new carrots leave them whole. Cover and for a further 2 hours continue to simmer so that the daube barely bubbles. Add the potatoes and continue simmering for 1 more hour. Skim off the excess fat and stir in the persillade. Serve, garnished with toast or French bread baked golden in the oven.

LANGUE DE BOEUF FARCIE
Stuffed Tongue Served with Broad Beans

1 salted ox tongue
1 oz dried *or* ¼lb fresh mushrooms
2 onions
1 egg
1 tablespoonful rillettes
1 tablespoonful breadcrumbs
2 carrots
2 rashers unsmoked streaky bacon
1 tablespoonful flour
2½ oz butter
1 tablespoonful tomato purée
1 claret glass Madeira

The bouillon

1 onion stuck with a clove
1 carrot
a stick of celery
a bouquet garni
6 peppercorns

Serves 4 to 6

De-salt the tongue in cold water for 12 hours. Put in a large pan, cover with fresh cold water, bring to the boil slowly and skim. Add the bouillon ingredients and boil gently for $3\frac{1}{2}$ to 4 hours. Cool in the liquid and then skin it. Trim off the bones, the fat and the horny parts. Cut out a rectangular block about 3 inches long from the thickest part of the tongue at the top. Cut a thin slice from the block and set aside—this will cover the stuffing in the tongue. Chop the rest very finely and mix with the rillettes, one of the onions finely chopped, the breadcrumbs and the mushrooms. If you are using dried mushrooms, soak them, just covered in warm water, for 30 minutes, then drain them, reserving the liquid, and chop finely. If using fresh mushrooms, chop them and simmer for 5 minutes in three tablespoonfuls of water to which you have added a squeeze of lemon and a nut of butter. Drain, reserving the liquid. Season the stuffing with the salt, pepper, herbs and nutmeg and stir in the egg. Stuff the hollowed out part of the tongue, cover with the reserved slice and tie round with string, curling the end of the tongue round as you do so.

Melt 1 ounce of the butter in a casserole and brown the sliced onion and carrots and the diced bacon in it. Put in the tongue and brown this carefully on both sides. Remove meat and vegetables to a plate and sprinkle the flour into the pan. Cook, stirring for a minute, then add the tomato purée, the liquid from the mushrooms and half a pint of the bouillon. Put back the meat and vegetables, cover and braise for $1\frac{1}{4}$ hours. Remove the tongue to a serving dish, cut the strings and keep warm. Put the rest of the contents of the pan through a sieve or the fine mesh of the food mill. Taste for seasoning and add the Madeira. Heat through gently and at the last minute add the remaining half ounce of butter. Serve the tongue with some of the sauce spooned over and the rest in a sauce boat, and accompanied by buttered broad beans.

GIGOT AU GENIEVRE
Lamb with Juniper Berries

1 leg of lamb, boned
3 tablespoonfuls juniper berries
1 tablespoonful good dripping
6 tablespoonfuls salt water

Serves 4 to 6

Trim off excess fat from the lamb. Crush two tablespoonfuls of the berries and stick them into the meat, studding it all over. Roll up and tie it and envelop in muslin. Hang in a cool airy spot for 4 days—in summer it is advisable to hang it for 2 days only. Untie it, smear the dripping over and roast on a rack in the oven with the salt water and the rest of the berries in the bottom of the pan. Baste often. To serve, carve the meat into thin slices, strain the juices in the pan and then reheat, scraping up the residue of meat juice from the bottom of the pan. Spoon some of the gravy over the meat slices and serve the rest separately.

FOIE DE VEAU OU DE MOUTON A LA TANTE LUCIENNE
Roast Liver in Madeira Sauce

1½ lb calf's or lamb's liver cut in 1 piece
½ lb unsmoked fat bacon cut in thin slices
½ pint Madeira sauce
1 clove garlic

Serves 4

Blanch the bacon for 5 minutes in boiling water, drain and

60

refresh under cold water. Pat dry. Season the liver with a little salt and some freshly milled black pepper and wrap it up in the slices of bacon. Roast in a moderate to hot oven, Gas 5—375°F, allowing 20 minutes to the pound. Baste with the juices in the pan. Unwrap and keep warm. Skim off excess fat from the pan juices, add the Madeira sauce and the chopped garlic, and let the sauce bubble for a couple of minutes. Carve the liver into thin slices and serve with a little of the sauce spooned over and the rest separate. See that the serving dish and sauceboat are hot.

BREZOLLES DE VEAU AGENAIS
Veal with Wine and Herbs

1½ lb veal cut in very thin slices from the
    inside of the leg
    a handful each of parsley and chives
    a few tarragon leaves
4 sprigs thyme
2 onions
4 rashers unsmoked streaky bacon
4 tablespoonfuls white wine
2 oz butter
    salt and pepper

Serves 4

Chop finely together the parsley, chives, tarragon, thyme and onions. Melt 1 ounce of the butter in the bottom of a pan and scatter a layer of the herbs and onions over it. Cover with a layer of the veal, place a few dots of butter over the meat, add another layer of the herbs and onions and then another layer of veal Continue these layers, seasoning with salt and pepper and placing a few dots of butter here and there until all is used up, finishing with a layer of herbs. Cover with the bacon rashers.

61

Put a piece of buttered paper over the top and then the lid of the pan. Cook very slowly for 1 hour. Add the wine, cover with the paper and the lid and cook a further 30 minutes. Remove the meat to a serving dish and keep hot. Skim off the excess fat from the juices, reduce the sauce for 2 or 3 minutes and serve poured over the veal.

ROTI DE VEAU QUERCYNOISE
Veal Roasted with Tomato and Garlic

2½–3 lb piece of roasting veal
½ pint white wine
4 tablespoonfuls oil
1 sliced carrot
1 sliced onion
4 cloves garlic
thyme, parsley and a bayleaf
a few peppercorns
5 or 6 ripe tomatoes

Serves 4 to 6

Marinate the veal for 12 hours in the white wine and the oil, together with the carrot, onion, two cloves of garlic, herbs and peppercorns. Then roast it, allowing 30 minutes to the pound. Halfway through the cooking time add the sieved tomatoes and the other two crushed cloves of garlic and continue roasting, basting with the juices in the pan and a few spoonfuls of the marinade.

RAGOUT DE VEAU AUX SALSIFIS
Veal with Salsify and Tomatoes

1½ lb breast or shoulder of veal cut into bite sized cubes

1 lb salsify
1 onion
1½ lb peeled and chopped tomatoes
1½ pints stock made from the bones of the veal
1 sprig thyme
1 bayleaf
1 sprig parsley
salt and pepper
1 oz good chicken, duck or goose fat or pure
beef dripping

Serves 4

Peel the salsify and cut into 1 inch lengths, putting each piece into a bowl of slightly acidulated water. Cut the veal into pieces, melt the fat and turn the veal in it, frying gently until the meat is golden. Remove with a slotted spoon, and to the fat in the pan add the drained and dried salsify and the onion cut into fine slices. Fry gently for 3 or 4 minutes, and meanwhile chop the tomatoes until they are almost reduced to a purée. Put the veal back into the pan and add the tomatoes and the stock, which should just cover the meat. Season with salt and pepper and add the herbs. Cook covered on a very low flame for 2 hours. Thicken the sauce with a little cornflour mixed with a little water to a smooth cream. Serve with noodles or thin macaroni.

RIS DE VEAU A LA TOMATE ET AUX CAPRES
Sweetbreads with Capers

3 pairs of sweetbreads
1 onion
1½ oz butter
1 clove garlic

63

$\frac{3}{4}$ pint beefstock and tomato sauce mixed
together (half and half)
2 tablespoonfuls capers
salt and pepper

Serves 4 to 6

Put the sweetbreads to soak in cold water for at least three
hours, changing the water at least twice. Blanch them by covering with fresh cold water, bringing them to the boil and simmering for 5 minutes. Drain and rinse in cold water. Trim them and
put them on a board in between two pieces of greaseproof paper,
place a weighted plate on top and leave for 2 hours.

Roll the sweetbreads in flour. Chop the onion and soften it in
the butter. Remove with a slotted spoon to a dish and add the
sweetbreads to the fat in the pan. When they are golden all over,
add the onion, chopped garlic, stock and tomato sauce. Season
with salt and black pepper and cook very gently for 1 hour, with
the lid of the pan tilted so that the steam escapes. Add the
capers 10 minutes before serving. Serve with a little chopped
parsley sprinkled over the top and with steamed new potatoes.

LES COTELETTES DE NONTRON
Pork Chops with White Wine, Garlic and Parsley

4 pork chops
2 tablespoonfuls pork fat
1 heaped tablespoonful breadcrumbs
1 tablespoonful chopped parsley
2 cloves garlic, finely chopped
6 fluid oz white wine
salt and pepper

Serves 4

Fry the chops in a heavy pan in half the fat with salt and pepper for 30 minutes, turning them after 15 minutes and keeping the flame low and the lid on the pan. Remove to a dish and keep warm, pour off the fat and add the white wine. Turn up the heat and let the wine bubble fiercely for a minute or two while you scrape up the residue and the meat juices to amalgamate them with the wine. Have ready in a separate pan the breadcrumbs and garlic fried in the rest of the fat until golden brown. Stir in the parsley and scatter over the chops. Pour over them the sauce made with the wine and serve very hot with mashed potatoes, and garnished with rounds of gherkin.

L'ENCHAUD PERIGOURDIN
Cold Boned Loin of Pork

3 lb loin of pork
3 cloves garlic
2 pig's trotters
$\frac{1}{4}$ pint meat stock
2 sprigs each of thyme and parsley
1 bayleaf
1 tablespoonful pork fat
salt and pepper

Serves 6

Have the loin boned and the rind removed. Cut the garlic into very small slivers and place them here and there all over the meat. Season with salt and pepper, roll up the loin and tie it with string. Put it in the refrigerator overnight. The next day, melt the pork fat in a heavy casserole or cocotte. Add the meat and the well scrubbed trotters and turn in the fat until they are golden. Add the herbs, cover and transfer to a low oven, Gas 3—335°F, for 3 hours. Add the meat stock and continue cooking at the same oven temperature for 1 more hour. Put the meat into an earthenware terrine, skim off the excess fat from the sauce and strain over the meat. Cool and remove the rest of the fat, which will have risen to the top.

The enchaud is served cold, cut in slices and with a little of the jelly for each person, often as an hors d'oeuvres, but it is very good as a main dish accompanied by salad. The pig's trotters are rolled in egg and breadcrumbs and grilled.

POULTRY

LE COU FARCI A L'OSEILLE
Stuffed Goose or Duck Neck with Sorrel

Serves 4

Turn the stuffed goose or duck neck slowly in the fat which adheres to it after taking it out of the confit pot. Make a purée of sorrel, put the neck in the saucepan with the vegetable and simmer for 5 minutes. To serve, cut in slices and arrange on the purée.

This is one of the oldest and best known of all Périgourdin dishes, which is served in the spring and early summer when the sorrel is young and tender. *Petits pois* cooked in the French way, with butter, tiny onions and a lettuce heart cut into strips, can replace the sorrel should it be unobtainable.

POULET DORE AUX CAPRES
Chicken with Capers

1 frying chicken jointed into 8 pieces
2 eggs
¼ pint of milk

1 lemon
3 shallots
2 cloves garlic
6 tablespoonfuls oil
2 tablespoonfuls butter
1 tablespoonful capers
4 tablespoonfuls white wine
  breadcrumbs
  salt and pepper

Serves 4 to 6

Beat up the eggs, the milk and the juice of the lemon together. Season with salt and pepper and leave the chicken pieces to marinate in the mixture for 3 hours, turning the pieces often. Drain and roll in the breadcrumbs. Peel and slice the garlic and shallots and soften them in the butter and oil. Add the chicken pieces and fry them very gently until they are

cooked through and until the juices no longer run red when the pieces are pierced with a fork. Take care to see that they do not burn.

When cooked, pile them up in a pyramid on a serving dish and keep warm. Pour off the excess fat from the pan and add the white wine. Reduce the sauce a little, stirring so that the wine and juices amalgamate. Add the capers and pour over the chicken pieces. This dish is also excellent if done with small thinly cut veal escalops, but in this case, omit the capers and serve garnished with lemon slices and parsley.

POULET SAUCE ROUILLEUSE
Chicken with Onions in a 'Rusty' Sauce

Recipe from the Café Restaurant at Celles

This is one of the classic dishes of the Périgord, but it is really practical only for those who keep their own chickens.

  1 cockerel or roasting chicken of $3\frac{1}{2}$lb
  2 tablespoonfuls goose or duck fat
  4 oz fresh pork—use either lean belly or spare rib
  2 tablespoonfuls flour
$1\frac{1}{2}$ pints water
  3 cloves garlic
 12 little onions
    a few drops of vinegar
    salt and pepper

Serves 4 to 6

The cockerel or chicken must be freshly killed and its blood collected in a bowl. Add the vinegar to the blood and put aside. Joint the bird and brown it all over in the fat in a heavy cocotte. Add the onions, the pork cut into tiny dice, and the chopped

68

garlic, and sprinkle the flour over. Bring the water to the boil and add gradually, stirring to make a smooth sauce. Season with salt and pepper and cook slowly on top of the stove for 1 hour, or until the chicken is tender. Then add the blood to the sauce and cook without boiling for 5 minutes. Serve immediately.

At the Café Restaurant Madame told me that just before serving she adds a tablespoonful of vermouth to the sauce (which is a delicious touch, but not classic).

LA POULE AU FARCI NOIR
Chicken with 'Black' Stuffing

This is another dish for those who keep their own chickens.

1 boiling hen
$\frac{1}{4}$ lb fresh minced pork
3 onions
2 cloves garlic
2 oz fresh white breadcrumbs
1 egg
1 tablespoonful chopped parsley
2 carrots
2 turnips
2 leeks
2 sticks of celery
2 cloves
  salt and pepper
  thyme and a bayleaf
2 tablespoonfuls butter

Serves 4 to 6

Mix the pork in a bowl with the chicken liver, finely chopped, the garlic and 1 of the onions chopped, the parsley and the egg.

Add the breadcrumbs, salt and pepper and, if you are using a freshly killed chicken, the blood. Stuff the chicken and sew up the openings. Turn it carefully in the butter in a large deep saucepan, and then add the vegetables and the onions, each stuck with a clove, the herbs, salt and pepper. Cover with boiling water and skim. Simmer very gently until the chicken is tender. Serve the soup first and then the chicken with the vegetables all round it. Generally a sauce vinaigrette aux oeufs is served with this, but I have also had it served with a mayonnaise into which a spoonful of capers and chopped walnuts was stirred.

The blood added to the stuffing is the local Périgourdine variation of a dish common to the whole of south-west France, but it can be dispensed with.

POULARDE EN CROUTE A LA MODE QUERCYNOISE
Chicken Pie with Salsify

Recipe from Monsieur Escorbiac

This is a dish which used to be made for special occasions and at holiday times, such as Carnival, when it was traditionally eaten in the Quercy. In the old days it was baked in the cast iron *tourtières* (three legged pots which stood in the embers of the fire) and glowing charcoal pieces were placed on the top. In the Périgord, where another version of this dish is made which includes tomatoes instead of the cream and eggs, many cooks bake the whole of the pastry shell first in round metal moulds and put the chicken and salsify in at the last minute, having first cut off the top of the cooked pastry to make a lid. But this method needs a lot of practice, especially in taking the cooked pastry shell out of the mould without damaging it. I am therefore giving the easier method as described to me by Monsieur Escorbiac of Cahors.

1 chicken of 2 to 2½lb (drawn and dressed weight)
2 lb salsify
6 tablespoonfuls cream
2 egg yolks
1 clove garlic
1 tablespoonful chopped parsley
½ lemon
salt and pepper
1 onion stuck with 2 cloves
2 carrots
a bouquet garni
1 lb flaky pastry

Serves 4 to 6

Put the chicken in a saucepan with the carrots and onion and the bouquet garni. Cover with water, bring to the boil and skim. Simmer until the chicken is tender. When cool, skin and bone it, keeping the pieces of meat as large as possible. Scrape the salsify, cut into 2½ inch lengths and boil until just tender in the chicken stock. Drain, reserving ½ pint of the stock for the sauce. With this stock, make a fairly thick bechamel sauce and add the chicken pieces, salsify, crushed garlic parsley and cream, then season with salt and pepper, bring to the boil and cook for 2 minutes. Off the heat add the egg yolks beaten up with the juice of the lemon. Let the mixture get quite cold.

Line a pie dish with just over half the pastry, allowing for 1 inch to overlap the edge of the dish. Put in the chicken and salsify and cover with the rest of the pastry, bringing up the overlapping edge to make a border. Brush over with a little milk and cut a slit in the centre to allow the steam to escape. Bake in a fairly hot oven, Gas 6—400°F, for 20 minutes, then turn down the oven to Gas 4—355°F and continue baking for another 25 minutes. Cover with a piece of foil if the pastry begins to get too dark on the top. Macaroni, cut into short lengths, can replace the salsify when it is no longer in season.

FOIES DE VOLAILLE AU MAIS
Chicken Livers in Red Wine with Sweet Corn

        1 lb chicken livers
        4 rashers unsmoked streaky bacon
       12 silverskin or pickling onions
        2 cloves garlic
        1 tablespoonful flour
       1½ oz butter
        1 teaspoonful sugar
          a pinch of quatre épices or nutmeg
          a bouquet garni
        6 fluid oz chicken stock
        6 fluid oz red wine
          salt and pepper

Serves 4

Make the sauce first. Brown the onions in 1oz of the butter, add the sugar and let this caramelise for a minute, then sprinkle the flour over it. Add the warmed red wine and the stock and stir until the sauce is smooth. Season with salt and pepper, add the bouquet garni, the crushed garlic and the spice. Simmer over a low flame for 40 minutes, stirring from time to time. 15 minutes before the sauce is cooked, fry the diced bacon gently in a heavy pan until the fat begins to run. Add the remaining butter and the cleaned livers and fry gently for 8 to 10 minutes, or until they are tender and cooked through but still pinkish inside. Drain off excess fat and add the sauce. Simmer for 5 minutes

72

with the sauce barely shuddering, and serve on a purée of sweet corn.

LE CANARD AUX DIGNONS
Duck with Onions

1 duck weighing 4 to 5lb before drawing and
   dressing
$\frac{1}{4}$ lb diced salt pork
24 silverskin or pickling onions
$\frac{1}{2}$ pint stock made from the giblets of the bird
1 glass white wine
2 tablespoonfuls olive oil
$\frac{1}{2}$ lemon

Serves 4 to 6

Season the cavity of the trussed duck with salt and pepper and place its liver and the half lemon inside. Brown it carefully all over in olive oil, prick the skin with a fork and put it in a dry baking tin in a hot oven, Gas 6—400°F, for 10 minutes. Meanwhile brown the onions in the same oil and put them in a heavy braising pan or cocotte, large enough to fit the duck comfortably without too much room to spare. Add the duck, moisten with a ladleful of the stock, season with salt and pepper and braise on top of the stove for $1\frac{1}{2}$ hours.

Pour off as much fat as possible from the juices (if you have a bulb baster, this will syphon it off very easily) and then transfer the pan minus its lid to the oven, Gas 5—375°F for 10 to 15 minutes to crisp up the breast of the bird. Put it on a serving dish with the onions and pork arranged all round and keep warm. Skim off any remaining fat and add another ladleful of stock and the white wine. Turn up the heat and let the sauce boil fiercely for 4 or 5 minutes, while you scrape up the meat

73

and onion juices and any crusty bits left on the bottom, amalgamating them with the stock and wine. Pour into a heated sauceboat.

GALANTINE DE CANARD VIALAR
Duck Galantine

Recipe from Madame Vialar of Vindrac

1 duck
1 lb minced pork
2 oz foie gras
4 oz chicken livers
1 egg
  a pinch of thyme
  a finely crushed bayleaf
$\frac{1}{4}$ teaspoonful pepper
2 truffles (optional)
3 dessertspoonfuls brandy
1 onion
2 carrots
  slices of pork back fat
2 claret glasses of white wine

Serves 4 to 6

Bone the duck, leaving only the drumstick bones. Cut off the breast fillets. Rub it all over with a little salt and pepper and a pinch of mixed spice and leave it in a bowl, together with the fillets and two dessertspoonfuls of the brandy, for 2 hours. Put the pork, chicken and duck livers through the fine blade of the mincer. Pound it in a mortar and add the egg, the pepper and thyme, the bayleaf, the sliced truffles, the rest of the brandy and a little salt. Spread half the mixture on the duck, lay the

74

flattened fillets on top and cover with the rest of the stuffing. Draw the edges together and sew up with fine thread. Wrap up the duck in the back fat and put it on a rack in a roasting tin, the bottom of which you have covered with the sliced onion and carrots. Pour over a glass of white wine and roast for 1 hour in a fairly hot oven, basting with the juices in the pan.

Madame Vialar, who runs a very small but highly reputed restaurant at Vindrac near Cordes, serves this galantine both hot and cold. If serving it hot, first remove the slices of pork fat 15 minutes before the duck has finished roasting, to crisp and brown the breast. Remove to a serving dish, cover and keep warm. Pour off all the fat and strain the remaining juices. Add the rest of the wine and half a pint of stock made from the bones and giblets. Reduce by fast boiling, taste for seasoning and serve with the duck. To serve the duck cold, make an aspic jelly (see page 198). Leave the duck to cool wrapped in its back fat slices, and when it is quite cold remove them and scrape off the fat from the skin. Brush over the duck twice with the almost set jelly and place on a serving dish. Chop the remaining jelly when it has set and arrange it round the bird.

PIGEONS AUX ASPERGES
Pigeons Casseroled with Asparagus

 4 pigeons
 3 oz belly of pork
16 pickling onions
 2 cloves garlic
 1 lb asparagus tips about 3 inches long
 $\frac{1}{4}$ pint red wine
 2 oz butter
 1 oz flour, salt, pepper
   a bouquet garni

Serves 4

Blanch the asparagus 5 minutes in boiling salted water. Drain and reserve ¼ pint of the water. Dice the pork and brown it, with the garlic and the onions, in the butter. Add the pigeons and turn them carefully in the fat until golden all over. Remove with a slotted spoon to a dish. Sprinkle the flour into the casserole and add the wine and asparagus water gradually. Put back the pigeons, pork, onions and asparagus. Season with salt and pepper and add the bouquet garni.

Cover with a piece of buttered paper and the lid of the casserole and simmer very gently for 1½ hours. Arrange the pigeons, onions and asparagus on a serving dish and keep warm. Skim excess fat from the juices in the pan, reduce the sauce for 2 or 3 minutes, correct the seasoning if necessary and pour over the birds. Serve surrounded by triangles of fried bread.

CAILLES A LA SUZON
Quails Baked in Potatoes

4 quails
4 baking potatoes
¼ lb minced pork
1 small shallot
1 truffle
2 tablespoonfuls goose fat or butter
3 tablespoonfuls meat or game stock
parsley and thyme
salt and pepper

Serves 4

Have the quails cleaned but with their heads left on and buy the largest baking potatoes you can find, rounded rather than oval in shape. Mix the pork with the very finely chopped shallot and the sliced truffle. Season with a little thyme and parsley, salt and pepper. Peel the potatoes, cut off a thin slice at one end and hollow them out until you have only a shell, large enough to take the quails. Put a small spoonful of the stuffing into each potato and the rest inside each quail. Melt the fat and turn the potatoes in it and then the quails until they are golden all over. Then put the birds into the potatoes, pushing them down carefully until only their necks and heads remain exposed. Put them upright into a casserole. Add the stock to the juices in the pan, let it bubble for a minute or two and pour over the potatoes. Cover and bake in a moderate oven, Gas 4—355°F, for 1 hour. Remove the lid, wrap the heads of the quails in foil to prevent them burning and continue baking for 1 more hour, basting with the juices. Just before serving, pour a few drops of Madeira over each quail.

This is a fantasy which should not be taken too seriously, but even if field mushrooms or cèpes are substituted for the truffle, it is a good and original way of dealing with quails or any other very small game birds.

CAKES, SWEETS AND PRESERVES

Acacia Flower Fritters

Acacia trees, which grow all over the Dordogne, flower in the spring, and these fritters, piled up on large dishes, are often served to guests after supper to eat with little biscuits and coffee.

fritter batter
4 oz sifted flour
   a pinch of salt
1 egg, separated
3 tablespoonfuls oil

2 teaspoonfuls orange flower water
1 tablespoonful brandy or rum
just under $\frac{1}{4}$ pint water

Serves 4 to 6

Mix the flour, salt and oil together. Add the beaten egg yolk, orange flower water, cognac or rum and, last, the water. Leave to rest for 2 hours and just before using stir in the stiffly beaten egg white. Pick the acacia flowers when in full blossom and make sure there is about 1 inch of stalk left on them. Holding them by the stalk, rinse them, dip them into the batter and plunge them into a deep pan of boiling oil. They will need only a minute or so to cook. Drain them on kitchen paper and serve with sugar sprinkled over them. Do not try to do too many at the same time.

If you have an elderberry tree in the garden, the flowers which blossom in May can also be successfully treated in the same way.

CREME AUX AMANDES
Almond and Orange-flower Water Cream

$1\frac{1}{2}$ pints milk
2 oz flour
4 eggs
1 teaspoonful almond essence
2 teaspoonfuls orange-flower water
1 tablespoonful sugar
1 oz blanched almonds
caramel made with 3 tablespoonfuls sugar and 1 dessertspoonful water

Serves 4

78

Mix the flour, eggs and sugar together in a bowl. Bring the milk and almond essence to the boil, cook slightly and strain on to the eggs and flour, stirring all the time. Cook in the top of a double saucepan over hot, but not boiling, water, until the mixture is thick and all taste of raw flour has been eliminated. Stir in the orange-flower water and pour the cream into a glass dish or into individual dishes. Refrigerate overnight. Garnish the next day with the almonds after dipping them into the caramel.

LA CAJASSE SARLADAISE
Rum Batter Cake

$\frac{1}{2}$ lb flour
  a pinch of salt
2 tablespoonfuls rum
5 oz sugar
$\frac{3}{4}$ pint milk
3 eggs

Sift the flour with the salt, add the rum, sugar, eggs and milk, stirring vigorously all the time. Pour the mixture into a buttered cake tin or soufflé dish. Keep stirring right up until you put it into a hot oven, Gas 6—400°F. Cook for 25 to 30 minutes. The cake should rise very high.

There is no one more conservative than a French peasant and perhaps those in the south-west of France, although their politics may be radical, are amongst the most conservative—particularly when it comes to food. It is, for instance, often extremely difficult to convince them of the merits of regional cookery in other parts of France. How often I have been told flatly, when discussing another province, 'They don't know how to cook there', and on disputing this and asking whether the speaker has ever been there or tasted the cooking, have received the reply, 'No, but from what I have heard they can't know how to cook. In any case, they don't eat as we do.' Nonetheless these eating habits, as everywhere in the Western world, are changing.

One thing, however, stubbornly remains the same for the peasant in the Quercy. He will have nothing to do with the long baguettes of bread produced by most bakers today. To him they are not real bread and he remains faithful to the enor-

The bread oven

mous round loaves, weighing several pounds each, and often at least a foot and a half in diameter, known as *tourtes*. He eats this bread in considerable quantities, hacking off chunks at meals with his knife, which he keeps in his pocket and carries around with him all the time; and woe betide his wife if she has run out of *tourtes* and has to use a smaller loaf with which to 'tremper la soupe'—pour the soup over the large thin slices at the bottom of the tureen.

When I visited one baker in the little village of Vaillac in the centre of the Lot, I had to wait until he had finished putting his loaves into the oven for the morning delivery. This was a really old bakery in the cellar under a mill and the unbaked loaves, about sixty in all, were lined up and covered with cloths on long trestle tables. They were turned out of their wooden baskets, dusted with flour and had a few gashes made in them with a knife before being put on long shovels and pushed into the old-fashioned log-fired oven.

It was this baker who gave me the following recipe for *coques*.

COQUES
Lemon Cakes
The Quercynoise version of Hot Cross Buns

1 lb 2oz flour
$\frac{1}{2}$ oz yeast
4 tablespoonfuls lukewarm water
$2\frac{1}{2}$ oz sugar
a pinch of salt
$2\frac{1}{2}$ oz butter
3 eggs and 1 extra yolk
grated rind of 2 lemons and 2 teaspoonfuls of the juice
1 teaspoonful rum

Serves 4 to 6

Dissolve the yeast in the water and mix it with $4\frac{1}{2}$ ounces of the flour. Cover with a cloth and leave in a warm place to rise for 2 hours.

Sift the rest of the flour with the salt into a bowl and add the sugar. Then gradually mix in the softened butter, the whole eggs, the grated lemon rind, 2 teaspoonfuls of the juice and the teaspoonful of rum. Beat the mixture well, using the dough hook of the electric mixer if you have one. Add the yeast mixture and knead the dough lightly on a floured board until it is smooth and elastic. This should not take long and the paste must not be overworked. Form into the shape of a loaf or into small rounds. Leave standing for 2 hours. Brush over with a beaten egg yolk and mark a cross on the *coques* with the back of a knife. Bake in a moderate oven, Gas 4—355°F, for 40 minutes if you are baking a loaf and for 20 minutes for little rounds.

They are eaten with jam and washed down with plenty of good white wine.

COURONNE AGENAISE
Chilled Rice with Fruit Stewed in Wine

    4 oz rice
    6 oz sugar
    1 vanilla pod
    1 pint milk
    $\frac{1}{2}$ pint whipped cream
    1 oz candied peel
    1 dessertspoonful rum
    $\frac{1}{2}$ oz gelatine melted in 3 tablespoonfuls
       warm water
    1 lb prunes or cherries
    $\frac{1}{4}$ pint red wine
    $\frac{1}{4}$ pint water
       cinnamon
    4 tablespoonfuls apricot jam
       angelica for decoration

Serves 4 to 6

82

Simmer the rice in the milk with the vanilla pod until tender but not mushy. Drain off any excess milk and add 3 ounces of sugar, the candied peel and the rum. Dissolve the gelatine and fold into the rice. Lastly add the cream. Put the mixture into a ring mould and chill until set.

Stew the prunes or cherries in the wine and water, together with the rest of the sugar and cinnamon. Leave to cool and mix in the jam. Unmould the rice ring, and decorate the top with small pieces of angelica. Put some of the fruit in the centre and serve the rest separately.

CROQUANTS DE MIEL
Honey Biscuits

10 oz plain flour
4 oz sugar
2 oz butter
2 eggs
1 tablespoonful honey

Serves 6

Rub the butter into the sifted flour and sugar. Add the eggs and knead on a board until the dough is smooth and no longer sticky. Roll out very thinly, stamp into rounds or cut into fancy shapes. Warm the honey until it is liquid and brush over the biscuits. Bake for 12 to 15 minutes in a moderate oven, Gas 4—355°F. Cool on a rack.

LA FOUACE DE QUERCY
Hearth Cake

This used to be made with cornmeal, but unless you can find some ground as fine as flour, use ordinary plain flour.

> 1 lb flour
> 3 eggs
> 5 oz sugar
> ½ oz yeast
> 3 fluid oz milk
> 1 tablespoonful cognac
> 1 tablespoonful orange-flower water
> 3½ oz butter
> a pinch of salt

Decoration
> 1 egg white
> 1 dessertspoonful orange-flower water
> granulated sugar

Dissolve the yeast in the lukewarm milk. Sift the flour with the salt into a large bowl. Make a well in the centre and add the sugar, the eggs one by one, the cognac, the orange-flower water and the yeast. Finally add the creamed butter. Knead the paste for 15 minutes until it is very supple. Roll into a ball, sprinkle with flour and cover with a cloth. Leave to rest in a draught-free room overnight. The next day, form into a ring and place on a buttered baking sheet. Leave for 2 hours and bake in a moderate oven, Gas 4—355°F, for 1 hour.

For the decoration beat 1 egg white and 1 tablespoonful of orange-flower water together and brush over the cake while it is still warm. Sprinkle with granulated sugar.

COMPOTE DE FRAISES ET CERISES AU VIN
Cherries and Strawberries in Red Wine

2 lb strawberries
½ lb red cherries
2 oz sugar
½ pint red wine
a pinch of cinnamon

Serves 4 to 6

Mix the wine, sugar and cinnamon together and pour over the hulled strawberries. Leave to macerate in a cold place for 2 hours. Strain off ¾ pint of the juice and cook the stoned cherries in it for a few minutes until tender. Add when cold to the berries. Serve the compote very cold with little biscuits.

PAVE AUX FRAISES ET FRAMBOISES
Raspberry and Strawberry Pudding

1 pint of milk
½ lb raspberries
½ lb strawberries
5 oz sugar
4 eggs
1 vanilla pod
28 sponge fingers

Serves 4

Bring the milk to the boil with the sugar and vanilla, turn off the heat and leave to infuse for 15 minutes. Beat the eggs and strain the hot milk over them, mixing carefully. Butter a soufflé or ovenproof dish and put a layer of the sponge fingers on the bottom. Pour half the milk and eggs over and then add the hulled and washed fruit. Cover with another layer of the sponge fingers and then add the rest of the milk and eggs. Bake, standing in a pan of water, in a fairly hot oven, Gas 5—375°F, for 45 to 50 minutes or until the mixture has set. Serve very cold.

LES MERVEILLES AND LES OGUILHETS
Fritters

At festivals and in the markets before holidays, such as Carnival and Easter, there is usually at least one stall where these fritters are cooked in great iron pots of boiling oil. At home it seems to be the special prerogative of Grandma to cook them and serve them up, sprinkled with sugar, to the children.

$9\frac{1}{2}$ oz flour
2 tablespoonfuls oil
3 eggs
1 oz sugar
$2\frac{1}{2}$ dessertspoonfuls each of rum and
    lukewarm water
    a pinch of salt
    oil for deep frying

Serves 4 to 6

Sift the flour and salt together into a bowl. Make a well in the centre and drop in the eggs, sugar and oil. Mix well with a wooden spoon and add the rum and water. Work the paste well, beating with the spoon and then with your hands until you have a smooth, slightly elastic dough, which leaves the side of the bowl. Turn out on to a board and knead again for a few minutes. Roll out as thinly as possible, cut into rectangles, squares or rounds and drop into boiling hot oil. The fritters will puff up and turn a deep golden brown. Drain on kitchen paper and serve with caster sugar sprinkled thickly over them.

In the local patois these fritters are known as *Les Merveilles* when they are cut into squares or rectangles; cut into rounds, they are called *Les Oguilhets*.

LE MASSEPAIN PERIGOURDIN
Périgourdine Sponge Cake

$2\frac{1}{2}$ oz flour
$2\frac{1}{2}$ oz granulated sugar
4 eggs
1 small teaspoonful orange-flower water
$\frac{1}{2}$ teaspoonful baking powder

Serves 4

Beat the sugar and egg yolks together until they are thick and fluffy. Gradually add the flour sifted with the baking powder and stir in the orange-flower water. Fold in the stiffly beaten egg whites. Pour into a buttered cake tin and bake at Gas 4—355°F for 35 to 40 minutes. The cake should rise very high. Cool and sprinkle with sugar.

The *massepain* is eaten on holidays and when there are guests, and is usually accompanied by a vanilla flavoured egg custard or Oeufs à la Neige (see page 88).

MILLASSE
Upside Down Pudding

4 eggs
2 oz flour
1 oz sugar
½ pint milk
1 vanilla pod
1 teaspoonful almond essence
caramel made with 3oz sugar and
4 tablespoonfuls water

Serves 4

Make the caramel first and line a greased metal or glass mould with it. Bring the milk to the boil with the vanilla, turn off the heat, cover and allow to infuse for 10 minutes. Mix the egg yolks with the flour, sugar and almond essence, and add the strained milk gradually, stirring all the time to avoid lumps. Whip the egg whites to a stiff snow and fold them in delicately. Pour into the mould and cook, standing in a pan of water, in a moderate oven, Gas 4—355°F, for 45 minutes or until a fine knitting needle plunged into the centre comes out clean. Cool slightly and turn out.

OEUFS A LA NEIGE AU CHOCOLAT
Chocolate Egg Snowball

6 eggs
¼ lb slab of plain chocolate
1½ pints milk
4 oz sugar

Serves 4

88

Separate the eggs and beat the whites very stiff. Melt the chocolate in a bowl over a pan of hot water. Bring the milk to simmering point and add the egg whites. Flatten the egg white mass slightly with a palette knife and try to keep it shaped like a round flat cake. Poach it gently in the simmering milk for a few minutes, flip it over with a large palette knife or fish slice and poach the other side. Leave to drain on a clean cloth. Beat up the egg yolks together with half the sugar and the melted chocolate in a bowl and pour the slightly cooled milk over the mixture. Place in the top of a double saucepan, the bottom half of the pan filled with hot but not boiling water. Place over the fire and cook, stirring constantly until the mixture has thickened to the consistency of thin cream. On no account let the water in the bottom of the saucepan boil. Pour into a glass bowl and place the poached egg whites on the top. Chill. Melt the sugar in a thick saucepan 10 minutes before serving and boil until it caramelises. Pour the caramel over the egg whites.

Oeufs à la Neige is also very often made with a vanilla flavoured cream instead of chocolate. Infuse a split vanilla pod in the milk for 10 minutes before adding the egg whites and substitute vanilla sugar for the plain when beating it with the yolks.

LE PASTIS QUERCYNOISE
Apple Cake

Every different region of the south-west of France has its own version of the *pastis*. One kind is a rather heavy cake made in the Aveyron with goose fat, another in the Basque country is made with a brioche dough, and there is this one of the Quercy which is very similar in ingredients, method and flavour to the central European *Apfelstrudel*.

1 lb flour
2 eggs

1½ oz butter
½ teaspoonful baking powder

Filling

3 lb apples
½ lb sugar
4 fluid oz rum
3 fluid oz orange-flower water
thinly pared rind of lemon

Peel, core and slice the apples very thinly and macerate them overnight with the lemon rind in the sugar, rum and orange-flower water. Sift the flour and baking powder into a large bowl. Make a well in the centre and add the eggs and the creamed butter. Mix lightly with the fingertips, drawing the flour over the eggs and butter, and gradually adding 7 fluid ounces of the liquid from the apples as you work the paste. Then beat the paste with your hand as for a brioche dough until it is smooth and elastic. Leave to rest for 1½ to 2 hours.

Roll it out carefully on a lightly floured board as thinly as possible and then transfer it to a floured cloth on a large table. Working from the centre and using the palms of your hands, begin pulling it out until it is as thin as cigarette paper, being very careful not to tear the dough. Leave to rest for 1 hour. Brush over with a little melted butter and dust lightly with sugar. Cover with the well drained apples and roll it up, tilting the cloth as you roll. Then roll it into a spiral and place in a large round buttered cake tin. Beat up one egg with the rest of the juice from the apples and brush over the top of the cake. Bake for 50 to 55 minutes in a fairly hot oven, Gas 5½—390°F, turning the tin after 25 minutes so that the cake cooks evenly.

The Périgourdine variation takes the form of a filled tart in which 3 or 4 discs of the same paste, each brushed over with a little melted butter or goose fat, are placed on top of each other in the bottom of the tin. The fruit, which can be apples, pears

90

or plums, flavoured with sugar and rum, is arranged on the top
and covered with two more discs of paste. Pastry trimmings are
cut into 1½ inch strips, curled and arranged over the top so that
it looks like a giant overblown tea-rose. After baking, the tart is
brushed over with a caramel.

CONFITURE DE FIGUES
Fig Jam

4 lb green or purple figs
3 lb sugar
¾ pint water
2 lemons

Wash the figs and leave them to drain. Cut off the small stems
at the top (but do not peel them) and then cut the figs in half.
Slice the lemons very thinly and cut into slivers. Dissolve the
sugar in the water and boil until small beads appear on the
surface. Add the figs and lemons and cook slowly for 3 hours, or
until the mixture thickens and a small amount sets when cooled
quickly on a saucer. Stir from time to time to prevent the jam
from sticking. Pour into warm jars and seal when quite cold.

PATE DE PRUNES
Plum Paste

2 lb plums
1½ lb sugar
1 teaspoonful cinnamon

Buy the little purple cooking plums known as *zwetchen* or
zwitzers, and see that they are quite sound and not too ripe. Wash

and dry them well and then peel and stone them. Rub them through a sieve—nylon if possible—and put them in a heavy preserving pan. Add the sugar and cinnamon and cook slowly, stirring constantly until they are thick and dark and beginning to candy round the edges. Pour the paste on to an oiled marble slab and leave for 48 hours. Then put it into very lightly oiled shallow tins, mark out squares or rectangles with a knife and dry out all day or overnight in the bottom of the lowest possible oven, Gas $\frac{1}{4}$—240°F. If you have a plate warming drawer underneath the stove, put them in there. They must remain for at least 12 hours. Roll them in granulated sugar and put them in tin boxes lined with good quality white paper, with paper in between each layer.

This is also delicious when made with freshly picked raspberries. Drain them really well before rubbing through the sieve and take an equal weight in sugar to the purée.

REINES-CLAUDE A L'EAU DE VIE
Greengages in Eau de Vie

Recipe from Madame Laffat of St Martial Viveyrols

4 lb greengages
2 lb loaf or preserving sugar
$\frac{1}{4}$ pint water
brandy, eau de vie de marc or vodka

The fruit should be only just ripe and still very firm. Wipe it and plunge into boiling water for 2 minutes. Then put immediately into cold water. Melt the sugar with the water and boil until the syrup has thickened slightly. Cool and, when quite cold, add to the greengages in a jar or stone crock. Top up with the alcohol. Seal the jar or crock and leave for 2 months before eating.

92

CONFITURE DE MELON AUX ORANGES
Orange and Melon Jam

4 lb water melon (weight when peeled
and with the seeds removed)
3 oranges
4 lb sugar
1 lemon
1 teaspoonful ginger
1 teaspoonful cinnamon

Cut the melon in small pieces and slice the oranges thinly.
Macerate for 24 hours together with the sugar and the spices.
Cook very slowly for 8 hours, stirring often. Pot and seal when
quite cold.

CONFITURE DE FRAISES ET DE RHUBARB
Rhubarb and Strawberry Jam

2 lb strawberries
2 lb rhubarb
3 lb preserving sugar
1 lemon

Hull, wash and dry the berries and leave to macerate in a
china bowl with half the sugar for 24 hours. Peel, wash and cut
the rhubarb into 1 inch lengths, add the rest of the sugar and
leave these also for 24 hours.

Cook the rhubarb and its juice for 10 minutes, together with
the juice of the lemon and its pips tied together in a little
muslin bag. Add the berries with their juice and boil for 15 to
20 minutes until the jam sets. Remove the bag with the pips and
ladle into warm sterilised jars. Seal when quite cold.

CONFITURE DE TOMATES VERTES
Green Tomato Jam

2 lb green tomatoes
1¼ lb preserving sugar
4 tablespoonfuls water
1 vanilla stick
2 lemons
1 liqueur glass brandy or rum

Wash and dry the fruit. Slice it and put it in a bowl with the sugar to stand for 24 hours. Put it in a preserving pan with its juices and the water. Cook gently for 10 minutes, add the vanilla stick, the juice and the grated peel of the lemons and boil fast until the jam begins to thicken. Add the rum or brandy and continue cooking until the jam sets. Ladle into small jars and seal when quite cold. This recipe makes a small quantity but it is not eaten on bread. In the Quercy where I came across it, it was served on saucers with little biscuits to accompany after-dinner coffee.

Chapter Three

AUTUMN

TO MANY, autumn is a season often tinged with sadness. But here in south-west France, it is often a time of rejoicing: of hard work certainly, for the big wine, maize and tobacco harvests fall at this time of the year; but also a time for cosy gatherings round the fireside to sort out and crack the best walnuts and to dry the maize, and while everyone works, the first chestnuts are roasted in the fire and the new wine savoured.

One very old lady in the little village of Le Grand Castang told me that it used to be the custom to tie the all-but-cooked chestnuts in a coarse linen bag and pass it round to each member of the party in turn, each having to sit on it for ten minutes and tell a story. If anyone failed to do so, he forfeited his next glass of wine.

Although the fierce heat of the summer is over, it is often still pleasantly warm and sunny and the nights are not yet too cool. The russet and deep-gold tints of the trees contrast with the paler gold of the maize and the yellowy green of the vines,

Cooking chestnuts

recalling the paintings of Van Gogh. The farmers hasten to pick the grapes, harvest the maize and tobacco and gather the nuts in great sacks to be taken to the presses for their oil. If they are not cracked for oil, the walnuts are spread out on slats of wood to dry in the sun before being stored away for the winter and early spring. For home use they are cracked on the big oak or cherrywood tables with a wooden hammer or mallet—which accounts for the holes in the table tops—or by the older people as they sit in the chairs in front of the fire, with trays on their knees.

So far as the local cookery is concerned, autumn is the great season for mushrooms and game. It is the time of *la chasse*, which, to the average Frenchman, does not mean hunting on horseback but shooting, often indiscriminately, at any bird, hare, rabbit or other animal that comes his way, in the hope that the victim will be some kind of game to be taken home with pride. In the private homes and restaurants, the game will be stuffed and roasted, turned into rich civets or stews or made into galantines and pâtés to take pride of place on the menus. If people are

Cracking walnuts with a mallet

not out shooting they are mushrooming, and this occupation and *la chasse* form the biggest topics for conversation in September and October. It is almost incredible how high feelings run when it is discovered that someone—more often than not a neighbour or one of his family—has stolen into your woods and gathered the cèpes and girolles whose existence you had so carefully concealed. If these mushrooms are not eaten fresh in omelettes and stuffings or fried with garlic, parsley and ham, they are tinned or bottled in large glass jars.

Although the Périgord is not one of the great wine-growing areas of France, it is too near the Bordeaux region not to produce some excellent wines, notably the Bergerac ones, of which the best known are the red le Pécharmont and the white Monbazillac, widely exported. This sweet white wine is said to be the only one drunk by Frederick the Great of Prussia, and that on the advice of his doctor—a fact which delighted the monarch's cook, who was a native of the Périgord. It was also exported in great quantities to the United Provinces, who called it the *Madeira of Périgord*.

From the Lot further south comes the *Vin de Cahors*, a wine of which the inhabitants of the Quercy are justly proud. At its best it is dark and full-bodied, with a slightly burnt flavour. Little known outside France except by experts, it is a wine with an ancient history, being exported to Rome under Caesar, and being greatly appreciated by those English serving in Aquitaine when that area formed part of the English possessions under the Crown. Apart from the wines of Bergerac and Cahors, however, most of the wine produced in the Périgord and the Quercy is for local or domestic consumption.

Those who have picked the grapes for wine in a good year will have experienced the sense of satisfaction that comes from such activity when the harvest is plentiful. The year I was asked to help out with a neighbour's harvesting promised exceptional wine, both in quantity and quality. When I arrived, on an unusually hot morning, work was already well ahead. The coloured straw hats of the women and the men's berets bobbed up and down as they knelt to snip off the bunches and fill their baskets. These were emptied into large containers strapped on to the backs of porters, who passed up and down between the rows of vines and then, with their backs bent under the load, staggered off down the hill to the wine press. This was being worked by two men who, I suspect, judging from the amount they found time to drink, had the easiest job of the day. In the small communes outside the wine growing areas of Bergerac and Cahors, the farmer grows grapes for his own consumption and invites his friends to help pick them, in contrast to the expensive vineyards of Bordeaux and Bergerac, where large numbers of students and casual workers are drafted in to gather the harvest. Thus it was a gathering of neighbours and relations who gossiped, joked and sang songs in the local patois as they worked till midday.

In the kitchen Madame had been busy all morning, and by the time we had finished our aperitifs the traditional soup served at harvest time, made from beef and vegetables slowly simmered in a rich stock enriched with wine, was on the long trestle tables set up in the courtyard outside the house. The beef and vegetables were served separately after the soup and were followed by guinea fowl, roasted and stuffed with mushrooms, little pieces of the fat local cured ham, garlic and herbs. Curiously, all the men gravitated to one table and the women to another, so that we sat segregated until one fat and jolly peasant lady got up in the middle of the meal and vigorously protested. Only a very short siesta under the trees was allowed us before we were hustled back to work, for it was hoped to finish this last vineyard by evening. About twenty-five of us worked solidly at snipping off the grapes until the final row was completed by about seven in the evening, as the sun was disappearing behind the hills. After a rest in the house came the party to celebrate the end of the harvest, with the traditional pancake-making and chestnut-roasting.

SOUPS

LA SOUPE DE LAPIN
Rabbit Soup

1 rabbit, jointed
2 onions stuck with a clove
2 turnips
2 carrots
1 leek
2 cloves garlic
1 tablespoonful flour
1 oz pork or goose fat or 2 tablespoonfuls oil
2 potatoes
1 sprig thyme
1 sprig parsley
1 bayleaf

The fricassée
2 finely sliced onions
1 slice ham diced
1 tablespoonful dripping

Serves 4 to 6

Turn the pieces of rabbit in the fat or oil for 10 minutes or until they are well browned. Add the vegetables, all except the potatoes finely sliced, and continue frying for a few minutes. Remove from the pan with a slotted spoon and sprinkle the flour into the remaining fat. When the mixture has taken on a little colour, add $5\frac{1}{2}$ pints of water gradually. Put back the rabbit and the vegetables, season with salt and pepper, add the herbs and simmer very gently for 2 hours, adding the potatoes cut into thick slices after the first hour. Fry the finely sliced onions and the ham together in the fat for the fricassée until the onions have taken on a little colour, and add to the soup. Cook again for 30 minutes. Serve the soup on slices of French bread baked in the oven and the pieces of rabbit with gherkins and a *sauce vinaigrette aux oeufs.*

TOURIN BLANCHI A L'AIL
Garlic Soup

1 tablespoonful pork or goose fat
6 cloves garlic chopped
1 tablespoonful flour
1 egg, separated
3 or 4 drops of vinegar
3 pints water
  salt and pepper

Serves 4

Fry the garlic in the fat until just golden. Add the flour and then the water gradually, so that there are no lumps. Season with salt and pepper, and bring to the boil. Add the egg white, and stir vigorously so that it separates into small pieces as it coagulates. Simmer for 30 minutes. Take the soup off the fire and add the egg yolk beaten up with the vinegar and a teaspoonful of cold water. The soup will thicken slightly. Serve with slices of French bread baked golden in the oven.

TOURIN AUX TOMATES
Tomato and Onion Soup

When there is a wedding in the town or village, this soup, champagne and little biscuits are carried up to the newly married

101

couple in their room on their wedding night and their friends, by this time considerably merry, stand round and force the unfortunate pair to drink it down. At least there is the champagne to follow and the soup is, if properly made, palatable, but in former days it was deliberately over-seasoned with pepper. In those days the bride was allowed to escape after having drunk one spoonful, but the poor bridegroom had to drink down the whole bowlful, to the accompaniment of ribald comments from his friends.

1 tablespoonful pork or goose fat
$\frac{1}{2}$ lb onions finely sliced
1 lb finely chopped peeled and deseeded tomatoes
1 crushed clove garlic
1 tablespoonful flour
  salt and pepper
1 bayleaf
1 sprig thyme
3 pints water

Serves 4 to 6

Put the onions to melt in the fat in a heavy pan. They will take about 20 minutes and should be watched and stirred from time to time to stop them from sticking. Sprinkle the flour over and stir well. Gradually add the water and then the herbs, and season with salt and pepper. Simmer for 30 minutes. Add the tomatoes and simmer for another 30 minutes. Serve with slices of French bread baked golden in the oven. About 3 tablespoonfuls of vermicelli are sometimes added to this soup 15 minutes before serving.

The Agenais variation on this uses fewer onions, replacing them with 3 or 4 potatoes, and the soup is sieved before the vermicelli is added.

LA SOUPE DES VENDANGES
Beef and Vegetable Soup

3 lb top rump or silverside
4 carrots
2 turnips
2 onions
1 cabbage cut into quarters
2 sticks celery
4 cloves garlic
3 tomatoes
  a bouquet garni
  salt and pepper
2 oz vermicelli
  a farci (see page 27)

Serves 6

Cover the beef with cold water, bring to the boil slowly and skim carefully. Add the carrots and turnips, peeled and sliced, the celery cut into pieces, the onions, tomatoes and garlic, and the bouquet garni. Season with salt and pepper and simmer extremely slowly for $3\frac{1}{2}$ to 4 hours. Add the vermicelli and the farci to the soup 20 minutes before serving. Serve the beef and the farci, cut in slices, after the soup. This soup, as its name indicates, is a traditional harvest dish; it is eaten at midday when the grapes are being picked.

SOUFFLES, VEGETABLES AND SALADS

SOUFFLE DE CELERI AU JAMBON
Celery and Ham Soufflé

1 lb cleaned celery
4 oz ham

103

3 oz grated cheese
4 eggs
2 tablespoonfuls butter
2 tablespoonfuls flour
¼ pint milk
   salt and pepper

Serves 4

Blanch the celery in salted water until it is just tender. Drain thoroughly, reserving a quarter of a pint of the cooking liquid, and cut into dice. Melt the butter in a heavy pan, add the flour and then the hot milk and celery water. Cook slowly, stirring all the time until the sauce is smooth and thick. Add 2oz of the cheese, and when this has melted, the egg yolks, beating them in one by one. Fold in the diced celery and season fairly highly with salt and freshly ground pepper.

Butter a soufflé dish and tie a band of paper round the top. Whip the egg whites until stiff and fold into the celery mixture. Place half the ham on the bottom of the dish, pour in half the mixture, add the rest of the ham and then the rest of the celery sauce. Scatter the remaining cheese over the top, dot with a little butter and bake in a preheated oven, Gas 4—355°F, for approximately 40 minutes.

GATEAU DE MORUE DE SAINT VINCENT
Salt Cod Baked with Potatoes and Walnuts

St Vincent is the patron saint of the winegrowers of south-west France, and this salt cod dish used to be eaten just after the harvest when the new wine was tasted. It was said to be one of the best accompaniments to the new wine because it made one so thirsty that one was forced to drink more.

104

1½ lb salt cod
1 lb potatoes
4 oz crushed walnuts
7 fluid oz walnut oil or arachid oil
6 eggs
1 clove garlic
   thyme and parsley

Serves 4

Soak the salt cod for 12 hours, changing the water frequently. Put it in a pan, cover with fresh cold water and bring it slowly to the boil. Take it off the heat and leave it in the water to swell and poach for 15 minutes. Boil the potatoes in their skins and mash them very smooth. Drain the fish thoroughly, skin and bone it, and flake it. Add to the mashed potatoes, together with the walnuts, the crushed garlic, the oil and the egg yolks. Season with pepper, a little thyme and parsley. Fold in the stiffly beaten egg whites. Pour into a lightly oiled soufflé dish or round cake tin and bake in a preheated oven, Gas 4/5—355°/375°F, for 40 minutes.

TARTE AUX NOIX DE PERIGORD
Périgourdine Nut Tart

3 oz chopped nuts
1 oz fresh breadcrumbs
4 tablespoonfuls chopped parsley
2 eggs
¼ pint milk
2 tablespoonfuls cream
6 oz shortcrust pastry

105

1 oz grated cheese
salt and pepper
a pinch of nutmeg

Serves 4

Line a tart tin with the pastry. Soak the breadcrumbs in a little water and then squeeze dry. Mix the nuts, breadcrumbs and parsley together and then add the eggs, previously beaten up together with the milk and cream. Season with the salt, pepper and nutmeg. Pour on to the pastry. Cover with the grated cheese, dot with butter and bake in the oven, Gas $4\frac{1}{2}$/5— 360°/375°F, for 40 to 45 minutes. Serve hot.

CHAMPIGNONS FARCIS
Stuffed Mushrooms

These should be prepared with large fresh cèpes, but the large flat mushrooms sold as field mushrooms are successful when treated in the same way.

8 large flat mushrooms
1 tablespoonful finely chopped ham
2 tablespoonfuls pork rillettes or minced fresh pork
2 tablespoonfuls chopped parsley
1 tablespoonful fresh white breadcrumbs
1 onion
2 cloves garlic
1 oz pork fat
1 egg yolk
6 tablespoonfuls tomato juice
a little oil

Serves 4

Clean the mushrooms, but do not peel them unless they are very dirty. Rinse them under the running tap, remove the stalks and pat the heads dry on a cloth. Chop the onion and fry it gently in the fat until it softens. Add the chopped mushroom stalks, the rillettes and ham, the crushed garlic, parsley and breadcrumbs. Mix well, and stir in the egg yolk, off the heat. Season with salt and pepper. Divide the mixture into eight and put a portion on each of the mushrooms. Oil a baking dish and put the mushrooms in. Moisten with the tomato juice, cover and bake in a slow oven, Gas 2/3—320°/335°F, for 30 minutes, removing the lid 5 minutes before the end. Baste often with the juices.

Cèpes

LES CEPES DE PERIGORD
Mushrooms Stewed with Garlic, Parsley and Ham

1 dozen cèpes
3 cloves garlic
3 oz raw unsmoked ham or mild gammon
a small handful of parsley

107

4 tablespoonfuls olive oil
pepper

Serves 4

Do not wash the cèpes. Scrape them well with a sharp knife
and then wipe them with a cloth. Cut off the stalks and chop
them with the garlic, parsley and ham to make an *hachis* mixture. Season with pepper. Put half the oil at the bottom of an
earthenware casserole, add a layer of the *hachis*, then the mushrooms and then cover with the rest of the *hachis*. Trickle the
rest of the oil over, put the lid on the casserole and cook for 2
hours on top of the stove with an asbestos mat under the pan.
Do not open the casserole during the cooking time.

POMMES DE TERRE AUX CEPES SECS
Potatoes with Dried Mushrooms

1 lb medium sized potatoes
3 oz dried mushrooms
2 fat cloves garlic
1 oz finely diced unsmoked streaky bacon or
salt pork
1 oz goose, duck or pork fat
2 tablespoonfuls chopped parsley
salt and pepper

Serves 4

Rinse the mushrooms under a running tap and then put them
to soak for 30 minutes in a pint of warm water. Drain, reserving
the liquid, and leave to dry on a cloth. Parboil the potatoes for
8 minutes in salted water, drain and cut into thickish slices.
Heat the fat in a heavy sauté or frying pan and add the diced

bacon or pork, the chopped parsley, the garlic and the mushrooms. Cover and cook slowly for 10 minutes. Add the potatoes, turn them for 2 or 3 minutes in the pan so that they are coated with the fat and mixed with the mushrooms and then add the mushroom liquid. Season with salt and pepper, cover and cook slowly for 35 to 40 minutes. There should still be a little liquid left at the end of the cooking time.

POMMES DE TERRE SARLADAISES
Truffled Potatoes

1½ lb potatoes
3 tablespoonfuls goose or duck fat
1 truffle
salt and pepper

Serves 4

Peel and slice the potatoes fairly thinly and evenly. Wash them in cold water and dry on a clean cloth. Brush the truffle, wash and dry carefully and cut into thin slices. Melt half the fat in a heavy frying pan. Put in the potatoes in layers, with slices of truffle in between the layers, and season with salt and pepper. Dot with the rest of the fat, cover the pan and fry gently on top of an asbestos mat for 30 minutes. The potatoes should have coagulated to form a galette or cake. Turn it over and continue cooking for another 15 minutes with the lid on the pan. For a more everyday version finely chopped ham, parsley and garlic may be used instead of truffles.

SALADE PERIGOURDINE ET QUERCYNOISE
Périgourdine and Quercynoise Salad

The Dordogne is France's largest walnut growing department

and a garden without at least one walnut tree is unthinkable. Practically every farmer has a walnut plantation on his land and the trees are to be seen growing everywhere—by the roadside, and in the fields among the maize, wheat and other crops. In the old days the oil was much more extensively used in the local cooking than it is now and most farmers had their own walnut presses. These have largely disappeared now and are only to be seen at the large fêtes which take place in the summer, where they add a little local colour and atmosphere. Nowadays the nuts are taken to the co-operatives in the nearest town, where they are then farmed out to local women to be graded, sorted and cracked. I have included few recipes which call for walnut oil, and I have also suggested substitutes. For this salad arachid oil can be substituted, but the result will not taste the same at all, since it is the seasoning with the walnut oil which gives the dish its purely local flavour.

   1 curly or Batavian endive
  12 walnuts
   6 tablespoonfuls walnut oil
   2 tablespoonfuls vinegar
    a slice of toast rubbed over on both sides
    with a piece of cut garlic

Serves 4

Wash the salad and shake it dry. Put the piece of toast in the bottom of the bowl with the salad leaves on top. Make the dressing with the oil, vinegar, salt and pepper and mix it in just before serving. Scatter the nuts over the top. Sometimes 2 hard-boiled eggs, cut into quarters, are added to make a more substantial salad.

SALADE DE CHAMPIGNONS QUERCYNOISE
Mushroom Salad Quercynoise

Choose large flat open mushrooms for this salad or, if you are living in the country and can find them, fresh field mushrooms. Allow 2 or 3 per person, bearing in mind that they will shrink during the cooking.

The rest of the ingredients are:

> 12 little pickling onions
> 2 sticks celery cut in small pieces
> 2 small lettuce hearts
> 2 large tomatoes
> 1 dessertspoonful tomato purée
> juice of 1 lemon
> 1 glass white wine
> a sprig of thyme
> 1 bayleaf
> 1 teaspoonful coriander seeds
> $\frac{1}{2}$ pint oil

Serves 4

Clean the mushrooms, chop the stalks and fry the heads and stalks in half the oil until they are soft. Drain well. Peel the onions, cut the lettuce hearts into quarters and slice the tomatoes. Put them in a pan with the lemon juice, tomato purée, herbs, wine, spice and the rest of the oil, season with salt and pepper and simmer for 25 minutes or until the onions are tender. Add the mushrooms and simmer for 5 minutes. Remove the mushrooms to a serving dish and boil the ingredients in the pan hard for 4 or 5 minutes. Pour over the mushrooms and serve very cold.

MEAT AND POULTRY

LA DAUBE DE CAUSSES
Beef Stewed with Wine and Mushrooms

$2\frac{1}{2}$ lb topside or round of beef in one piece
2 tablespoonfuls pork fat
4 cloves garlic
2 onions
$\frac{1}{4}$ lb streaky bacon
1 lb carrots
5 or 6 ripe tomatoes
2 oz dried mushrooms or $\frac{1}{2}$lb fresh mushrooms
$\frac{1}{2}$ pint good beef stock
$\frac{1}{2}$ pint red wine
salt and pepper
a bouquet garni
1 tablespoonful flour

Serves 6

Lard the beef with the bacon cut into strips and insert slivers of the garlic here and there into the meat. Brown it all over in the fat. Remove, and soften the onions in the fat. Sprinkle the flour over and cook for 2 minutes, then add the stock. Put back the meat and arrange the carrots, cleaned and cut into slices, all round. Pour the wine over and add the seasonings. Finally sieve the tomatoes through the coarse mesh of the food mill over the meat. Cook very slowly, Gas 1—290°/310°F, for 5 hours. Leave overnight. Next day, add the quartered mushrooms or soak the dried mushrooms in a little hot water until they are soft, drain away the liquid and add them to the daube. Cook again at the same temperature for another 2 hours. Serve with a very creamy purée of potatoes or with slices of French bread, toasted and rubbed over with garlic.

I have called this the *Daube de Causses* because although daubes are eaten all over the south-west of France and in Provence this particular version was given me by an old lady living in a practically deserted village on the Causse de Gramat in the Lot. It used to be cooked by her grandmother in a large copper pot and was the traditional dish left simmering on the hearth when the family went to market in the nearest town once a month. In other parts of the Lot, at Puy l'Evêque for instance, the *Daube* was traditionally eaten on All Saints' Day after the yearly visit to lay chrysanthemums on the family graves at the cemetery. On that day, in the old bourgeois families, the whole household including the servants sat down to lunch together.

VEAU FANCHETTE
Veal Braised with Breadcrumbs, Garlic and Parsley

2½ lb roasting veal from chump end of loin
4 tablespoonfuls breadcrumbs
¼ lb salt pork
2 shallots, finely chopped
2 tablespoonfuls parsley, finely chopped
2 cloves garlic, crushed
1 egg and 2 egg yolks
 pepper
4 carrots
2 onions
1½ oz butter or good dripping

Marinade
 oil and white wine
 pepper

1 bayleaf
thyme and parsley
1 clove garlic

Serves 4

Marinate the veal for 12 hours. Mince or chop the pork finely and mix with the breadcrumbs, shallots, parsley, garlic, the egg and the yolks together in a bowl and season highly with pepper. Pat the veal dry with a cloth or on kitchen paper and spread the *hachis* all over and round it, so that it is covered. Chill 1 hour in the refrigerator. Slice the carrots and the onions. Melt the fat in a cocotte and turn the meat in it, taking care to damage the *hachis* as little as possible. Add the carrots and onions, and moisten with a little of the marinade. Cover and braise extremely slowly for 2½ hours. Serve garnished with lemon slices.

DODINES DE VOLAILLE
Marinated Chicken Pieces Stuffed with Mushrooms and Chicken Livers

Ask the butcher or poulterer to bone a medium sized chicken for you. Cut the boned chicken into four pieces and flatten them with a cutlet bat.

4 pieces boned chicken
 a marinade made with white wine (see page 199)
1 bayleaf
 sprig of parsley
 sprig of thyme
 salt
5 peppercorns
2 tablespoons brandy

114

Stuffing

$\frac{1}{4}$ lb mushrooms
$\frac{1}{4}$ lb chicken livers
1 medium sized onion
2 rashers streaky bacon
1 clove garlic
$1\frac{1}{2}$ oz butter
1 tablespoonful brandy
salt, pepper, thyme and parsley

Braising mixture

1 tablespoonful butter or good fat
$\frac{1}{4}$ lb salt pork, diced
6 small onions
2 cloves garlic, chopped
2 carrots
a bouquet garni
1 claret glass Madeira

Serves 4

Chop the mushrooms, garlic and onions extremely fine and soften them in the butter, together with the finely diced bacon. Add the cleaned and chopped chicken livers and continue frying gently until the livers are browned but not completely cooked through. Mix with the salt, pepper, thyme, parsley and brandy. The stuffing should not be too sloppy, so if too much juice has exuded from the frying, strain some of it off. Cool slightly and stuff the chicken pieces with it, roll them up, tucking the ends in, and sew up all the openings so that none of the stuffing can escape. Put them in a bowl with the sliced carrots, onion, garlic, herbs and seasonings and pour the brandy and wine over them. Put a plate which will fit inside the bowl on top of them and a

2lb weight on the plate. Leave in the refrigerator for 3 to 4 days. Then braise them in the braising mixture.

Brown the diced salt pork and vegetables in the butter and remove to a dish. Turn the well-dried dodines in the rest of the fat carefully until they are golden on all sides, being careful not to pierce the skin. Remove. Sprinkle the flour over to make a roux and add the strained marinade juices. Bring to the boil, put back the vegetables and chicken pieces, add the bouquet garni and season with salt and pepper. Braise very gently for $1\frac{1}{2}$ hours. Remove the chicken pieces to a serving dish, cover and keep warm. Skim off excess fat and put the sauce and vegetables through the food mill. Add the Madeira and heat through gently. Pour over the chicken and serve.

POULET SAUTE AU VERJUS
Chicken with Grapes

1 frying chicken weighing about 2 to $2\frac{1}{2}$lb
2 onions
1 clove garlic
$\frac{3}{4}$ lb white grapes
$1\frac{1}{2}$ oz butter
2 tablespoonfuls olive oil
the juice of 1 small lemon
salt and pepper

Serves 4 to 6

Joint the chicken and fry it with the finely chopped onions and garlic in the olive oil and 1 ounce of the butter until it is tender and cooked through. Remove to a serving dish and keep warm. Meanwhile press half the grapes through a sieve to extract the juice and peel and deseed the other half. Fry the peeled grapes in the same fat quickly for 2 or 3 minutes and arrange round the chicken. Skim off the excess fat in the pan, add the grape and lemon juice and stir, scraping up the crusty residue round the edges and from the bottom of the pan. Correct the seasoning and whisk in the remaining $\frac{1}{2}$ ounce of butter. Pour over the chicken pieces and serve with chopped parsley scattered over the top, and fried potatoes.

CANARD VILLENEUVOIS
Duck with Prunes

1 duckling
1 lb prunes
2 onions
2 carrots
3 tablespoonfuls oil
6 rounds of fried bread
$\frac{1}{2}$ bottle red wine
1 liqueur glass brandy
    salt, pepper, thyme and a bayleaf

Serves 4 to 6

Soak the prunes for 1 hour, and blanch them for 5 minutes in lightly salted water. Heat the oil in a heavy pan, add the sliced onions and carrots and herbs and let them soften slowly for 10 minutes. Add the pounded liver of the duck, pour over the wine and season with salt and pepper. Simmer slowly for 20 minutes, then put through a sieve or the food mill. Add the brandy, and then the drained prunes. Simmer very slowly until they are tender. Remove from the fire. Take out half the prunes and stuff the duck with them. Roast the duck on its side in a fairly slow oven, Gas 3—335°F, for $1\frac{1}{4}$ hours, turning it over after the first 30 minutes and laying it breast side up for the last 15 minutes so that the skin crisps and browns. Baste occasionally with the juices in the pan. Put the bird on a serving dish. Heat up the sauce gently, arrange the rest of the prunes on the fried bread around the duck with a little of the sauce spooned over and serve very hot.

FILETS DE DINDE VENDANGEUSE
Turkey Breasts with Grapes and Artichoke Hearts

3 turkey breasts
1 onion
1 carrot
1 tablespoonful pork, goose or duck fat
6 cloves
2 slices unsmoked streaky bacon
½ pint chicken stock
1 tablespoonful cognac
6 artichoke hearts
½ lb green grapes

Serves 4 to 6

Flatten the turkey breasts and cut them in half so that you have six fillets. Remove any skin and stick small slivers of garlic and bacon into them all over. Line a sauté pan with the fat, the sliced onion and the carrot, put the turkey breasts on top and add the cloves and bouquet garni. Moisten with a tablespoonful of water and let this reduce completely. Add the stock, season with salt and pepper and place in a moderate oven. Cook for 25 minutes, basting frequently, by which time the breasts should be cooked through but still moist and tender. Meanwhile boil the artichoke hearts until tender and pip the grapes. Put the meat on a hot dish and keep warm. Skim off the excess fat, add the hearts and grapes to the juices in the pan and reduce the sauce by fierce cooking for a couple of minutes. Surround the

118

breasts with the hearts garnished with the grapes. Strain the sauce and spoon over the meat.

GAME

LES BECASSES DE LA BARONNE
Braised Stuffed Woodcock

Woodcock are usually served roasted without being drawn, their entrails being mashed at the last minute with salt, pepper and lemon juice, spread on slices of toast and served with the bird on the toast. This recipe, a very old one, makes a change.

 4 woodcock
 $\frac{1}{4}$ lb chicken livers
 1 dessertspoonful capers
 $\frac{1}{4}$ lb mushrooms
 2 shallots
 1 anchovy, previously rinsed under a
   running tap for a few minutes
 $\frac{1}{2}$ oz butter
 1 tablespoonful parsley
   salt and pepper
12 little white onions
 1 sliced carrot
 $\frac{3}{4}$ pint Madeira sauce

Serves 4

Make a stuffing with the entrails of the birds, the finely chopped chicken livers, capers, mushrooms and shallots. Add the parsley and butter, and season, taking into account the salt in the anchovy. Stuff the birds with the mixture and then braise them in a heavy cocotte with the little onions and carrot

119

arranged around and the Madeira sauce. Braise for 1 to 1½ hours until the birds are very tender, and serve them on rounds of French bread fried till crisp and golden and with the sauce poured over.

LAPIN FARCI SARLADAISE
Stuffed Roast Rabbit

1 young rabbit
2 oz good dripping
5 oz unsmoked streaky bacon
2 oz breadcrumbs
2 eggs
1 clove garlic
2 finely chopped shallots
1 tablespoonful chopped parsley
½ tablespoonful chopped chervil
1 large pinch finely chopped rosemary
    salt and pepper

Serves 4 to 6

Chop together the heart and liver of the rabbit with the bacon. Add the breadcrumbs, the shallots and crushed garlic, the herbs and the eggs. Season with salt and pepper. If the mixture seems too stiff, moisten with a very little water or bouillon. Stuff the rabbit with the mixture and sew it up. Smear half the dripping all over the rabbit and put the rest, with ¼ pint of water, in the bottom of a roasting pan. Wrap up the rabbit in two sheets of buttered greaseproof paper and roast in a moderate oven, Gas 4—355°F, for 1 hour, basting with the juices from the pan. Unwrap the rabbit, sprinkle a little salt over it and roast another 30 minutes, basting every 5 minutes. Serve with *pommes sarladaises* and a salad of walnuts and chicory or young dandelion leaves.

120

LAPIN EN PERSILLADE
Rabbit with Mustard, Parsley and Garlic

1 rabbit jointed
4 oz belly of pork
2 tablespoonfuls goose or pork fat
3 cloves garlic
2 tablespoonfuls strong French mustard
1 peeled and roughly chopped tomato
3 tablespoonfuls chopped parsley
4 fluid oz white wine

Serves 6

Brown the rabbit pieces and the diced belly of pork carefully in the fat. Add the mustard, finely chopped garlic, tomato and two tablespoons of the parsley. Season with salt and pepper, and pour the wine over. Cover the pan and simmer for 30 minutes or until the rabbit pieces are tender, stirring from time to time. Serve with the rest of the parsley scattered over the top.

This is also very good with veal instead of rabbit.

CIVET DE LIEVRE DUMONTEIL
Hare Stewed in Red Wine

Recipe from Madame Dumonteil of Riberac

1 hare
a marinade (see page 199)
¼ lb fresh belly of pork
¼ lb salt pork
2 onions
3 cloves garlic
2 shallots
2 tablespoonfuls chopped parsley
2 tablespoonfuls flour
1 sugar lump
a bouquet garni of thyme and bayleaf
a pinch of nutmeg
¾ bottle red wine
1 tablespoonful brandy
1 glass meat or game stock

Serves 4 to 6

Put the liver and blood of the hare in a small bowl with a teaspoon of vinegar and set aside. Joint the hare and marinate it overnight. Put the red wine in a pan with the shallots, the sugar lump, the bouquet garni and the nutmeg. Set it alight and simmer very gently for 1 hour. Dice the belly of pork and melt it in a heavy pan. Drain the pieces of hare, dry them, roll in flour and turn them in the fat from the pork. Chop together the onions, garlic, salt pork and parsley and add to the pan. Fry gently until they have taken on a little colour, then pour the red wine and stock over. Season with salt and pepper, cover and cook in a low oven, Gas 2/3—310°/335°F, for 1½ hours. Pour the brandy over and continue cooking a further 30 minutes. Crush the liver to a paste in a mortar and add the blood. Pour this into the casserole and simmer, stirring gently on top of the stove until the sauce is bound and thickened. Do not allow the sauce to boil. Serve, accompanied with garlic-rubbed croutons of fried bread or toast. Sometimes dried cèpes, previously soaked for 10 minutes, are added to the civet half-way through the cooking time.

Madame Dumonteil, who gave me the recipe for this particular civet, is proprietress of a *charcuterie* in Riberac in the Dordogne. I have named the recipe after her.

LIEVRE EN CABESSAL QUERCYNOISE
Pot Roasted Hare

The *cabessal* was a white cloth wound round into a spiral and then placed flat on the heads of the women to make anything they carried on their heads more comfortable. It was worn at harvest time when the filled baskets of picked grapes were carried down to the press at the bottom of the hill, and by the women living on the Causses, where water is often scarce, when carrying their filled pitchers back from the local pump.

  1 hare
  ½ lb fresh minced pork
  3 oz tin of mousse de foie or bloc foie gras
  2 cloves garlic
  1 tablespoonful parsley
  1 egg yolk
10 little pickling onions
  2 carrots
    rashers of unsmoked fat bacon or back
      fat for barding
    a marinade (see page 199)

Sauce
> the blood and liver of the hare
> 5 oz salt pork, belly if possible
> 5 oz shallots
> 2 cloves garlic
> ½ teaspoonful dried thyme
> 6 fluid oz vinegar

Serves 4 to 6

Make sure that the hare is kept whole and not jointed, and ask for the heart as well as the blood and liver. Put the liver and blood into a bowl with a few drops of vinegar and set aside in a cool place. Put the hare in the marinade and leave for 12 hours or overnight. Make a stuffing of the chopped heart, pork, mousse de foie, crushed garlic, chopped parsley and egg yolk. Season with salt and pepper. Wipe the hare inside and out with a cloth and stuff. Sew it up, tie the hind legs together at the end and form it into a round, pushing the head through the hind legs. Melt the fat in a heavy casserole and brown the onions and the sliced carrots. Remove to a dish and brown the hare carefully on both sides. Put back the vegetables, moisten with 3 table-spoonfuls of the marinade and lay the slices of back fat or bacon over the hare. Cover and pot roast gently for 2 hours, turning the hare over after 1 hour.

Meanwhile make the sauce. Dice the salt pork as small as possible and chop the shallots and garlic together until they are almost a purée. Cook them slowly together with the thyme for 10 minutes, keeping the pan covered. Add the vinegar and let this bubble fiercely for 2 or 3 minutes. Pound the liver until it is reduced to a purée in a mortar and mix with the blood. When the hare is cooked, remove it to a serving dish and keep warm. Skim off the excess fat from the juices in the casserole and add the vinegar and shallots. Bind the sauce with the pounded liver and the blood and heat through gently. A tablespoonful of red currant jelly can be added before the final binding should you find the sauce too sharp.

PERDRIX AU CHOUX
Partridge with Cabbage

 1 partridge
 1 fine large cabbage
 $\frac{1}{2}$ lb minced fresh pork
 1 or 2 truffles if possible
    or 3oz pâté de foie gras truffé
 2 shallots
 2 cloves garlic
    a little thyme and parsley
    a pinch of quatre épices
 2 egg yolks
 2 tablespoonfuls cognac
 12 silverskin or pickling onions
 2 oz goose, duck or pork fat
 1 tablespoonful flour
 4 thin slices of back fat for barding
 4 rashers of unsmoked streaky bacon
 $\frac{1}{2}$ pint meat or game stock made from giblets

Serves 2

Blanch the whole cabbage in boiling salted water for 10 minutes. Drain thoroughly and open it out leaf by leaf carefully until it resembles a large green flower. Cut out the heart. Clean the partridge but leave the liver inside the bird. Wrap it up in the slices of back pork fat and brown it carefully in a casserole in half the fat. Warm half the brandy in a spoon, set light to it

125

and flamber the partridge with it. Remove the bird to a dish and set aside while you make the stuffing.

Mix together the pork, finely chopped shallots and garlic, sliced truffles or pâté, egg yolks, spice, herbs and cognac. Season with salt and pepper. Put the partridge in the centre of the cabbage and then put a thin layer of the stuffing on each of the leaves until all is used up. Gather up the cabbage so that the bird is completely enclosed and tie well with tape. Add the rest of the fat to the casserole and turn the onions in it until they are golden. Sprinkle the flour over and simmer, stirring for 2 minutes, then moisten with the stock. Put in the cabbage with onions arranged all round, lay the pieces of bacon on the top and cover with a buttered piece of greaseproof paper or foil. Put on the lid and braise very slowly for 3 hours or put in the oven at Gas 2—310°F for the same amount of time.

LE CUISSOT DE CERF
Marinated Venison

a 6 or 7lb saddle of venison
a marinade (see page 199)
2 tablespoonfuls butter
2 tablespoonfuls oil
3 rashers streaky bacon
1 spoonful red-currant jelly

Serves 8 to 10

Place all the marinade ingredients in a large china or glass bowl and let the meat remain in the mixture for 10 days in a cool place. Turn it at least twice a day. At the end of 10 days, take out the meat, wipe it dry and lard it with the bacon. Brown it all over in the butter and oil and then roast, allowing 20 minutes to the pound and 20 minutes over, basting often with some of the marinade juices. Serve it with a creamy purée of chestnuts, celeriac or salsify.

This dish was the *plat d'honneur* when the Comte de Lamarcandie, a noted gastronome from the Dordogne, entertained. Only the best Chambertin was considered a worthy accompaniment to drink with the venison. Champagne was served in the salon after dinner while the guests held a raffle with the antlers as the prize.

ESCALOPES DE CHEVREUIL GRESIGNOISE
Venison Steaks Grésignoise

The Forest of Grésigne is a domanial forest just outside the old medieval town of Cordes, which is at the extreme south-east of the Quercy, bordering the Aveyron and Albigoise regions. The cooking is influenced by all three regions, olive oil and goose and duck fat being used and confits made; olives, which are rarely come across further north, go into sauces, stuffings and garnishes, and the sumptuous Cévennes game dishes of wild boar and venison are found on all the gastronomic menus in season.

4 thick venison steaks, from the haunch if
    possible
2 oz duck, goose or chicken fat
1 oz dried mushrooms
¼ pint game stock
1 tablespoonful brandy
2 tablespoonfuls port or Madeira
1 oz butter
    Slices of back fat or unsmoked fat bacon
      for barding
    a marinade (see page 199)

Serves 4

Marinate the steaks for at least 12 hours in the oil and wine, with the carrot, onion, herbs and juniper berries. Add salt and freshly ground black pepper and turn the meat occasionally. Drain and wipe dry. Soak the dried mushrooms for 20 minutes, drain and reserve $\frac{1}{4}$ pint of their soaking liquid. Bard the steaks and put them to roast with the fat and the dried mushrooms underneath them in a hot oven, Gas 6—400°F, for 15 to 20 minutes, basting frequently. Drain off all the fat, and flamber with the brandy. Add the stock, the mushroom liquid and the port or Madeira. Turn up the heat and let the sauce bubble for 1 or 2 minutes, spooning it over the meat. Put the steaks and mushrooms on a serving dish and keep warm. Continue reducing the sauce for a further 2 minutes and whisk in the butter, cut into pieces. Correct the seasoning and pour over the meat. Serve very hot.

CAKES, SWEETS AND PRESERVES

GATEAU BRANTOMOIS
Sultana Cake

3 eggs
2½ oz caster sugar
2½ oz fine breadcrumbs
2 tablespoonfuls sultanas previously soaked
in a dessertspoonful of rum
2 teaspoonfuls orange-flower water
rum syrup made as for the rum cake on page 193

Serves 4

Separate the eggs and mix the yolks, sugar, breadcrumbs and orange-flower water together in a bowl. Cover with a cloth and leave for 3 hours. Butter an 8in cake tin or ring mould. Beat the egg whites stiff and fold them together with the drained sultanas into the egg and breadcrumbs. Pour into the tin and bake for 35 to 40 minutes in a moderate oven, Gas 4—355°F. Turn out on to a rack and pour the syrup over while it is still hot.

GLACE AUX PRUNEAUX
Prune Ice-cream

3 egg yolks
2½ oz sugar
¾ gill water
¾ pint double cream
1 vanilla pod
12 oz prunes
3½ fluid oz brandy

Serves 4 to 6

Soak the prunes in the brandy overnight. Then cook them in the juices until tender. Stone them and chop the flesh very finely or put into the electric blender for approximately 1 minute.

Dissolve the sugar in the water over a low heat. Infuse the split vanilla pod in the cream over low heat for 20 minutes, then strain. When all the sugar has dissolved, bring to the boil and boil rapidly to the thread stage. Cool slightly and pour over the previously creamed egg yolks, whisking until the mixture is thick. Add the cream and then the prunes. Chill, then pour into the ice trays and freeze for ¾hr to an hour or until firm enough to beat. Turn the mixture into a bowl and beat hard, then return to the freezer or refrigerator and freeze till firm.

LOU CACAOU
Walnut Cake from the Périgord Noir

2 eggs
1 egg yolk
2 oz sugar
4 oz sifted flour
6 tablespoonfuls cream
1 teaspoonful baking powder
2½ oz crushed walnuts

Caramel

4 oz granulated sugar
½ gill water

Serves 4 to 6

Beat together the yolks and the sugar. Add the flour and then the cream and mix well; the mixture should drop easily from the spoon. Add the nuts, lifting the batter with the spoon as you fold them in. Pour into a buttered and floured cake tin and bake 35 minutes, Gas 5—375°F. Turn out on to a rack. Make a caramel with the sugar and the water and dip about 15 fresh nuts into it. Stick them on to the cake and then pour the caramel over the cake, smoothing it down with a knife dipped in hot water.

MILLIAS AUX POMMES
Pumpkin and Apple Cake

Pumpkin cake, made with maize flour or cornmeal, is a speciality common to much of the south-west of France. This particular version including apples was given me by a farmer's wife living just outside Les Eyzies in the Dordogne.

3 lb pumpkin
8 oz fine cornmeal
8 oz caster sugar
3 eggs, separated
4 oz butter
½ pint milk
3 tablespoonfuls rum or brandy
¾ lb apples

Serves 8

Peel the pumpkin, remove the seeds and cottony centre, cut into pieces and blanch in slightly salted boiling water for 10 minutes. Drain thoroughly and put through the coarse mesh of the food mill. Cut the butter into dice and add to the pumpkin. Mix well together and then add the sugar, rum, egg yolks and cornmeal. Mix well together and gradually add the milk. Peel, core and slice the apples thinly and add to the batter. Fold in the stiffly beaten egg whites. Butter a round cake tin—the one I use is 9½in in diameter. Pour in the batter and bake for 1 hour at Gas 5—375°F. Serve while still hot. Any leftovers can be cut into slices, rolled in sugar and fried in butter the next day.

GATEAU A' L'ORANGE ET NOISETTES
Orange and Hazelnut Cake

4½ oz sugar
4½ oz hazelnuts
3 eggs, separated

131

1 oz butter
1 orange
2 oz potato flour

Orange butter cream

4 oz unsalted butter
½ lb icing sugar
1 tablespoonful rum
   juice of 1 orange and its zest

Serves 4 to 6

Roast the nuts for a few minutes in a hot oven and as soon as they are cool enough to handle, rub off the skins. Crush them in a mortar or mince them finely. Beat the yolks till pale and fluffy, add the sugar, the potato flour, the minced nuts, the grated peel, the juice of the orange and the oiled butter. Mix well and fold in the stiffly beaten egg whites. Pour the batter into a buttered and floured ring mould and bake in a moderate oven, Gas 4—355°F, for 35 to 40 minutes. Cool on a rack and decorate with orange butter cream, made as follows

Beat the butter in a warmed bowl until creamy, and add the sifted sugar gradually, beating it well in. Add the rum, orange juice and zest. Spread this cream over the top of the cake and arrange a few more hazelnuts round it.

GATEAU RENVERSE AGENAIS
Prune and Apple Upside Down Cake

1 lb prunes
3 apples
5 oz flour
4½ oz butter

$4\frac{1}{2}$ oz sugar
$\frac{1}{4}$ pint milk
1 egg
1 teaspoonful baking powder

Serves 4 to 6

Soak the prunes for 1 hour and stone them. Peel, core and slice the apples. Cream 2 oz of the butter together with 2 oz of the sugar and spread over the bottom and sides of a cake tin. Line the bottom and sides of the tin completely with the prunes and apple slices. Cream together the rest of the butter and sugar, and alternately add the egg and then the milk and flour sifted with the baking powder. Pour the mixture into the tin and bake in the oven at Gas $5\frac{1}{2}$—385°F for 40 to 50 minutes or until a knitting needle plunged into the centre comes out clean. Cool slightly and turn out on to a serving dish. Serve warm with cream.

CREPES A L'ANIS
Aniseed Pancakes

Pancakes are eaten throughout the year in the Périgord and the Quercy, but especially during the winter and at Carnival time. In the old days, when they were made for the Carnival, the first one had to be cooked with the frying pan held in the right hand, while the woman held a piece of money—preferably a Louis d'or—in her left hand. After it was cooked, the pancake was tossed over her left shoulder in the hope that it would land against the wall above the dresser. All this was to bring luck and wealth on to the house throughout the coming year.

The first time I had these particular pancakes was at a party to celebrate the end of the wine harvest. They were cooked in pans over a log fire in the kitchen. The hostess mixed the batter in a large porcelain bowl with her bare hands because, she said,

133

it made the batter lighter; but it must be done deftly and with the tips of the fingers. As more liquid is added, the batter should be lifted with the hands and allowed to run through the fingers back into the bowl so as to incorporate as much air as possible.

8 oz flour
4 eggs
1 tablespoonful rum or brandy
1 tablespoonful milk
1 oz aniseed grains
1 dessertspoonful sugar
a pinch salt
between $\frac{1}{4}$ and $\frac{1}{2}$ pint water
$\frac{1}{2}$ an apple

Serves 6 to 8

Sift the flour into a roomy bowl with the salt. Make a well in the centre and break in the eggs. Begin working these together with the finger-tips of one hand and add the rum, milk and sugar. When you begin to have a very sticky dough, gradually add the water, beating it in with your hand. Lift up the batter from time to time and allow it to run through the fingers back into the bowl. You should end up with a light, creamy batter. Stir in the aniseed grains and leave to rest for at least 2 hours. Should it then have thickened too much add a little more water. Stick a fork or skewer into the rounded unpeeled side of the apple, dip it into oil and shake off the surplus. Rub it around the heated pan to grease it, pour in a little of the batter and make the pancakes in the usual way.

LES COINGS CONFITS
Quince Preserve

Quinces grow commonly all over the Périgord and the

134

Quercy. In the Périgord Agenais, quince trees were formerly used instead of fences to mark off the limits of each property in the same manner as laburnum trees were used further north in the Dordogne towards the Charente.

> 5 lb quinces
> 5 lb sugar

Wash the fruit, cut into quarters and then into eighths but do not peel. Cut out the cores but reserve the seeds and tie these in a muslin bag. Soak the fruit and seeds in cold water for 3 hours. Drain and take the equal weight in sugar. Put into a preserving pan, just cover with fresh cold water and simmer until the fruit is soft and almost transparent. This will take 7 hours. Remove the fruit with a slotted spoon and put into pots. Boil the syrup fast until setting point. Pour over the fruit and seal when quite cold.

LES PRUNEAUX ET NOIX FARCIS
Stuffed Prunes and Walnuts

> 20 walnuts
> 20 large prunes

Almond paste

> 4 oz ground almonds
> 3 oz icing sugar
> 2 teaspoonfuls brandy
> a little egg white or gum arabic

Caramel

> 5 oz loaf or granulated sugar
> water

Serves 4 to 6

135

Mix the first three ingredients together, and then add the gum arabic (which can be bought at most chemists) or about half the white of a small egg so that you end up with a smooth but fairly stiff paste. Colour, if you wish, with a few drops of cochineal or green food colouring.

Halve 20 walnuts and soak or steam 20 large prunes until they are tender enough to be stoned. Stick the two walnut halves together with a little of the paste in between, and stuff the prunes. Make a caramel by dissolving 5 ounces lump or granulated sugar in $\frac{1}{2}$ a gill of water and then boiling it until it is a good rich brown. Put a little on the top of each prune and dip the walnuts in it. Stand them on a lightly oiled marble slab or baking sheet to dry.

Chapter Four

WINTER

LATE November to the middle of January is the great season for preserving the geese and ducks and making the pâtés of goose and duck liver for which this region is so justly famous. The pâtés are usually tinned, the soldering on of the lids taking place at the local village general store or smithy whilst one waits. Then the tins are put in large cast-iron sterilising cauldrons, weighted down and boiled.

Most families make their pâtés a year in advance, for they say that in order to allow the flavour to develop to the full the pâté must mellow and ripen in a cool dark place for twelve months. The temptation to try them earlier usually proves too great, however, and by April or May the first ones have been opened, usually for Sunday lunch.

The *Marchés aux Gras* (or Geese and Duck Markets) present a fascinating sight during these winter months. It was bitterly cold, with ice on the roads and snow on the fields, when we arrived early one morning at Tocane, a small town in the

Dordogne, to buy our goose livers and to see if we could find someone selling truffles. In the market square the specially fattened ducks and geese, plucked and singed, were laid out on trestle tables, and the livers, pale rose and gold and resembling tropical fruit, presented an unreal aspect as they lay there neatly arranged and covered with greaseproof paper or white cloths to protect them from hardening in the icy wind. Prodding and examining the birds and the livers were the peasant women, dressed in black, with shawls round their heads and warm carpet slippers on their feet. Before a goose or duck was bought, its

A warm spot in the winter

back had to be slit open four or five inches so that the liver inside could be examined.

There were very few truffles around and those who had some were reluctant to sell them individually. The plastic bags in which the fungi were kept were brought out of baskets or satchels surreptitiously, as if the owners were afraid one might snatch them away without payment. Eventually we were able to persuade one man to sell us a single large truffle.

The winters in this part of France can be very cold, especially on the eastern hills and plateaux. But indoors it is warm. In the evenings the kitchen shutters are closed and the huge oak logs hiss and splutter in the fireplace. A large cast-iron pot, blackened with age and smoke, hangs from a hook in the chimney, the soup inside simmering slowly for the evening meal. By the side of the fire some sausages or slices of the local salted ham may be arranged on the grill, or perhaps a basket of eggs stands next to a pan of hot water in the corner of the hearth. The practice of cooking eggs in their shells in the embers after first having dipped them in the hot water is still common, and their flavour is much finer than that of eggs boiled in the ordinary way.

On Christmas Eve slices of black and white pudding are often grilled over the fire and eaten with drinks before dinner. While the truffled goose or turkey is roasting in the oven, Madame is decorating the table and arranging large platters of oysters and the foie gras, studded with slices of black truffle. On its dish on the dresser out of reach of the children, stands the yule log, made of chestnuts and chocolate and flanked by little bowls of biscuits, sweets and crystallised fruits.

The dinner takes place early in the evening, so that the whole family can go to Midnight Mass in the village church. In the old days, the carols were sung in the local dialect. When the family comes home again the presents are distributed and *le caboussat*, hot spiced wine, is drunk. If, when they get back, the fire is still alight, this is regarded as a good omen.

Towards the end of January and in February the pigs are killed. Specially cosseted and fattened during the preceding months, they grow to enormous sizes. The whole family is involved in the operation of killing, cleaning and cutting up the animals, almost every part of which is used. The hams are salted and hung up in linen bags to dry, the fat is melted down for lard, the loin is boned and preserved, and the intestines, after lengthy washing, form the casings for sausages and black and white puddings.

Many farmers keep more than one pig, and the largest is often killed for the Carnival. In the old days this was the time of year when the local people gorged themselves on meat—not just because of the Lenten fast which followed, but so as not to waste any part of the precious animal which could not be preserved. Many were too poor to be able to afford beef or lamb except on special occasions, such as Easter. So pig's trotters, roasts and daubes of pork, and little dishes of the ears and tail stewed in white wine appeared, followed by the traditional pancakes, sponge cakes and waffles. So ingrained is this custom that the old saying *Per cornobal, se majo de car* (One eats meat for the Carnival) is still heard several weeks beforehand in certain parts of the Lot.

SOUPS

LA SOUPE DE MARRONS
Chestnut Soup

> 2 lb chestnuts
> $\frac{1}{2}$ lb unsmoked streaky bacon cut into dice
> 1 carrot, sliced
> 1 potato cut into quarters
>   a bouquet garni
> 2 pints stock
> 2 cloves
> 2 tablespoonfuls breadcrumbs
> 2 egg yolks
>   salt and pepper

Serves 4 to 6

Shell the chestnuts, cover with cold water, bring to the boil and boil slowly until they are tender and the inner skin can be peeled off. Put the nuts in a pan with the bacon, vegetables, herbs, seasonings and stock. Boil steadily until the vegetables are tender. Put the soup through a sieve, add the breadcrumbs and heat through gently. Just before boiling point, whisk in the egg yolks. Serve the soup with croutons.

SOUPE DE JAMBON
Ham Soup

2 lb ham
2 leeks
2 carrots
2 onions
1 cabbage
3 oz vermicelli
   pepper and salt
4 cloves, 1 bayleaf
$\frac{1}{2}$ pint white wine

Serves 4 to 6

Put the ham, leeks, carrots and onions into a large pan. Cover with 3 pints of water, and add the white wine, the cloves, a good pinch of pepper and the bayleaf. Bring to the boil and simmer very gently for 2 hours. Add the cabbage cut into chunks and simmer for 1 more hour. Skim and add the vermicelli. Cook until the vermicelli is tender. Serve the soup first, and then the ham, which can be eaten hot with freshly boiled leeks, carrots and cabbage, or cold, cut into slices and garnished with hard-boiled eggs and little gherkins. With the ham serve a vinaigrette sauce, into which you have mixed plenty of chopped garlic, parsley and chives.

POTAGE QUERCYNOISE
Quercy Soup

2½ pints veal or beef stock
6 tomatoes
2 tablespoonfuls cream
2 tablespoonfuls vermicelli
1 slice cooked ham
2 sticks celery
2 egg yolks
1 bayleaf
1½ tablespoonfuls oil
1 pinch nutmeg
½ teaspoonful quatre épices
  salt and pepper

Serves 4 to 6

Cook the roughly chopped tomatoes in the oil until they are softened and then put them through the coarse mesh of your food mill into the hot stock. Add the cleaned and diced celery and the vermicelli and cook steadily for 20 minutes. Beat up the yolks with the cream and the spices and thicken the soup with the liaison. *Do not boil.* Add the diced ham and simmer below boiling for 2 or 3 minutes. Serve with little croutons of fried bread.

LA SOBRONADE
Vegetable Soup with Ham and Preserved Goose

This soup, also more prosaically called *La Soupe Epaisse* (thick soup), is one of the most common of all Périgourdine soups.

1 lb gammon or 1 lb salt pork
1 wing or leg of preserved goose or duck
½ lb haricot beans
1 cabbage
4 carrots
4 small turnips
4 medium sized potatoes
1 stick celery
3 onions
4 cloves garlic
  a bouquet garni
3 cloves
  a pinch of quatre épices
3 tablespoonfuls pork fat

Serves 4 to 6

Soak the beans overnight. Put them in a pan with water to cover them and bring to the boil. Turn off the heat and leave them for 30 minutes. Drain. Put them together with the gammon or salt pork in a saucepan and cover with fresh water. Bring to the boil and simmer slowly. Clean the cabbage and cut it into quarters. Peel and slice the other vegetables. Melt the pork fat in a frying pan and turn the carrots and turnips in it slowly until they have taken on a little colour. Add them to the soup with the celery, onions, potatoes, herbs and seasonings. Cook for 1 hour and add the piece of confit and the cabbage. Cook at simmering point another 2 hours.

Cut some slices of French bread thinly and put them in the bottom of your soup tureen 15 minutes before serving. Fry the remaining onion, finely sliced, with 1 clove of garlic and some parsley in a little pork fat and put this on top of the bread. Remove the gammon and the confit and pour the soup over the bread. The gammon and the confit are served after the soup.

EGGS, DUMPLINGS
AND STUFFED VEGETABLE DISHES

L'OMELETTE AUX TRUFFES
Truffle Omelette

With truffles such a price, outside France this is an omelette only for the epicures or the rich. Yet no book dealing with the cookery of the Périgord can leave it out, for it is a classic from the area and one which appears in the restaurants on all Menus Périgourdines.

> 1 truffle
> 1 oz butter
> 6 eggs
>   salt and pepper

Serves 4

Wash and brush the truffle carefully all over with a soft brush and then peel it thinly. Cut into thin slices. Melt half the butter

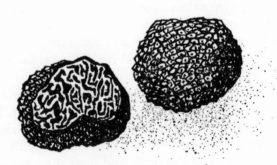

Truffles

144

in a small pan and add the truffle slices. Heat them through gently for 1 or 2 minutes, but take care that they do not harden or burn. Add them to the beaten eggs, well seasoned with salt and pepper, and make the omelette in the usual way with the rest of the butter. In the Périgord the butter would be replaced by goose fat, and some cooks add a few drops of cognac to the truffles while they are being heated in the fat.

OEUFS EN COCOTTE PERIGORD
Baked Eggs with Chicken and Périgueux Sauce

For each serving allow
    1 or 2 eggs
    1 tablespoonful diced cooked chicken or game
    2 tablespoonfuls sauce Périgueux

Butter as many ramekin dishes as there are people to serve and put a spoonful of the diced chicken or game at the bottom of each. Add half the sauce Périgeux and heat through gently in a moderate oven, Gas 4—355°F. When the chicken is hot, break the eggs over it carefully, cover with the rest of the sauce and dot with butter. Put the little dishes in a shallow pan filled with boiling water, which should come halfway up the side of the dishes. Bake in a fairly hot oven, Gas 5—375°F, for 8 to 10 minutes until the eggs have set.

LES OEUFS FARCIS
Deep Fried Stuffed Eggs

    1 hard-boiled egg per person
    1 extra egg, separated
    1 dessertspoonful minced cooked chicken or
        ham per egg
    1 clove garlic

1 tablespoonful each chopped parsley
and chives
salt and pepper
breadcrumbs
oil

Serves 4

Cut the hard-boiled eggs in half and with a sharp knife remove
the yolks, being careful not to damage the whites. Mix the yolks
with the ham or chicken, the herbs and the yolk of the extra egg.
Season with salt and pepper and stuff the whites with the mixture. Chill for 1 hour. Beat the white of the extra egg until
frothy, dip the eggs into it and then roll them in the breadcrumbs, coating them well all over. Fry in the boiling oil. Drain
on kitchen paper and serve with tomato sauce.

FARCIDURE DE QUERCY
Salt Pork with Dumplings

2 lb salt pork
1½ lb flour
3½ oz butter
3 eggs
a large pinch salt
½ oz yeast
2 onions
2 carrots
1 small cabbage

Serves 4 to 6

Dissolve the yeast in a teacupful of warm water and mix in a
bowl with the flour, the barely melted butter, the eggs and the

salt. Knead well until the dough is elastic and no longer sticks to the side of the bowl. Form into a ball, wrap in a floured cloth and leave to rest in a warm place for 3 hours. Put the salt pork on to cook, covered with fresh cold water in a large pan with the cleaned vegetables. Simmer it gently for at least $2\frac{1}{2}$ hours. 1 hour before you wish to serve the pork, add the farcidure, and turn it over halfway during the cooking time. Serve the soup first and the pork and farcidure afterwards. One old lady to whom I mentioned this recipe said that she added two large tablespoonfuls of rillettes to her farcidure, a variation of a dish eaten all over the Quercy.

LA MIQUE
Périgourdine Dumpling

Recipe from Madame Delpech

12 oz crusty bread, not too fresh
4 eggs
1 oz butter, or goose or pork fat
3 oz unsmoked fat bacon minced fine
5 oz cornmeal
   a vegetable bouillon
   salt and pepper
   a pinch of sugar

Serves 2 to 3

Cut the bread into little cubes and mix with the eggs, the butter, the bacon and the sugar. Season and then gradually add the cornmeal. Mix well. Flour your hands and form the mixture either into small dumplings or, as is more traditional, into one big one. Roll it in flour and simmer it for 30 minutes in a soup pot in good vegetable bouillon. The dumpling is very often served instead of bread with cabbage and ham soups, or to accompany a confit of goose or duck.

This recipe was given to me by Madame Delpech, who with her husband runs a small café tabac in a little village in the heart of the Périgord Noir. The café is clearly the main meeting place of the village, and nearly all the local housewives gathered there on the afternoon of my visit, as soon as news got around that I had gone to enquire about recipes.

POUNTI QUERCYNOISE
Gammon and Spinach Pie

5 oz gammon
1 lettuce or ½ lb spinach leaves
1 small handful parsley
1 medium onion
2 cloves garlic
5 oz flour
1 teaspoonful baking powder
3 eggs
¼ pint milk
  rashers of streaky bacon
  salt and pepper

Serves 4 to 6

Chop together the gammon, garlic, parsley, onion and lettuce or spinach. Stir in the eggs, then the flour sifted with the baking powder and finally the milk. Season with salt and plenty of black pepper. Line a pie dish or casserole (cast iron if possible) with the streaky bacon, pour in the mixture and bake in a fairly hot oven, Gas 5—375°F, for 1 hour. Serve cut in wedges with tomato sauce.

L'ALIGOT
Potatoes Puréed with Cheese and Cream

2 lb floury potatoes
12 oz cheese
3 oz butter
1 gill cream
1 fat clove garlic
  pepper

Serves 4

This is made with unfermented white Cantal cheese, known locally as *La Fourme*. Use a mild cheese which melts easily, such as Caerphilly.

Bake the potatoes in their skins and scoop out the pulp. Add the butter and the cream and put into a heavy pan over a low flame. Add the crushed garlic and the cheese cut into tiny pieces and season with freshly milled pepper. Whip the mixture until it is very light and fluffy, turn it quickly into an ovenproof dish and put in a hot oven, Gas 7—425°F, for 2 to 3 minutes.

LE PESCAJOUN DE SARRAZIN
Buckwheat and Potato Pancakes

1½ lb potatoes sliced thinly
3 cloves garlic
2 tablespoonfuls parsley
1 slice gammon diced
5 tablespoonfuls buckwheat
3 eggs
  milk and water
  salt and pepper
3 tablespoonfuls pork, goose or duck fat

Serves 4 to 6

149

Sauté the potatoes in a heavy frying pan with the chopped garlic, parsley and diced gammon. Keep the pan covered for the first 10 minutes and the heat low. Have ready a batter made with the buckwheat, eggs and enough milk and water to make it the consistency of a pancake batter. Leave it to rest for 1 hour. When the potatoes are soft but not reduced to a purée, add the batter to the pan and cook on both sides. If you wish, the potatoes can be added to the batter and ladlefuls cooked in the pan to make smaller pancakes.

CHOU FARCI A LA PERIGOURDINE
Stuffed Cabbage Périgourdine

1 large green cabbage
2 sliced carrots
4 shallots
1 large or 2 small tomatoes roughly chopped
$\frac{1}{4}$ lb unsmoked streaky bacon
1 gill white wine
  salt and pepper
  a piece of muslin or string netting large
  enough to enclose the cabbage when stuffed

Stuffing

$1\frac{1}{4}$ lb minced fresh pork
2 tablespoonfuls breadcrumbs
1 large onion, finely chopped
1 egg
$\frac{1}{4}$ lb flat open field or grilling mushrooms,
  or dried mushrooms soaked in a little
  hot stock
1 tablespoonful finely chopped parsley
2 crushed cloves garlic

150

1 crushed bayleaf
a pinch of thyme
a pinch of ground cloves
1 tablespoonful brandy

Serves 4

Blanch the cabbage, keeping it whole, in boiling salted water for 10 minutes. Drain thoroughly, cool and open it out leaf by leaf without detaching the leaves from the centre core. It will look like a large overblown green rose. Cut out the heart, chop it and mix with the stuffing. If you are using fresh mushrooms, wash them and wipe dry but do not peel them unless absolutely necessary. Cut off the sandy parts of the stalks, slice the mushrooms and simmer them in a pan with a little water and a nut of butter for a few minutes to get rid of excess moisture. Drain them and mix with all the stuffing ingredients in a bowl. Season rather highly with salt and freshly milled black pepper.

Put a thin layer of the stuffing on each leaf, and reconstitute the cabbage into its original shape. Tie it round with tape or fine twine and wrap it in the muslin or netting. Line the bottom of a heavy casserole with the bacon, put in the cabbage and place the carrots, tomatoes and shallots around. Pour over the white wine, place a piece of buttered paper on top and cover with the lid. Cook in a very slow oven, Gas 2—310°F, for 5 hours. Unwrap the cabbage carefully and turn it out on to a serving dish, arrange the slices of carrot, tomato, shallots and little pieces of bacon all around and pour the sauce over. Half the quantity of minced veal can be substituted for those who do not like an all pork stuffing.

TRUFFLES

Truffles have been mentioned as a delicacy from the earliest times, the Greek philosopher Theophrastus being the first to write about them in the 2nd century BC and Juvenal, Pliny and Plutarch also mentioning them. They were probably referring to the white truffle known as *terfez* imported from North Africa and the similar *kames* which grew in the sandy soil of Asia, for no mention of the black truffle occurs until much later.

The most prized black truffle for cooking is the one found in the Périgord and the Quercy, the *tuber melanosporum*, first mentioned in cookery books in the 15th century. It grows in lime soil particularly under oak and hazelnut trees, but its cultivation is extremely hazardous, depending as much on the weather and pure chance as any knowledge of growing methods. It takes at least ten years before the truffles begin to appear, and a good deal of rain is necessary. In the last few years the summers have been drier than usual, and this as well as deforestation accounts for much of the decline in production, though the Truffle Producing Syndicate in the Périgord is making great progress in replanting oaks and preserving truffle areas against development.

Truffles can be collected by various methods, of which the two best known are the use of pigs and dogs and what is called *La Récolte à la Mouche*. The latter is more commonly used by poachers nowadays and is more chancy. When ripe, the truffles are attacked by the larvae of a certain species of blowfly, which, before laying its eggs, hovers just above the truffle bed in the early morning and late afternoon, thus indicating the position of the fungus. Those who use this method often spend a considerable time lying on their stomachs in order to get a better view of the flies, which are very small. Where dogs and pigs are used, the animals are carefully trained to scent out the truffles, scrabbling and snuffling at the soil until they find one. Dogs are more easily trained to indicate the spot and then leave their master to dig the fungus out, but pigs, which are notoriously fond of them, have to be prevented from eating the precious harvest.

Pigs searching for truffles

The Périgord black truffle is not found in England or America, but another black species was hunted in England until the end of the Edwardian era. John Evelyn and Tancred both mention them growing at Rushton in Northamptonshire and Gilbert White's brother had some on his estate in the south of England. This English variety grew in beechwoods and in the chalky soil of Sussex, Hampshire and Wiltshire, and was hunted with dogs. A French doctor, who published a dissertation on truffles in 1766, mentioned the use of specially trained dogs in England and Rudyard Kiplin wrote a short story about an English truffle hound, as well as trying to cultivate them at Burwash. A similar species has been found in parts of California and Oregon.

153

I have included only one recipe for truffles because of their high price and the impossibility of obtaining fresh ones outside France. When fresh, they can be kept in moss for about a week and so retain their scent, but they do not travel very well and they lose part of their aroma and flavour when preserved in jars or tins. Yet I cannot omit them altogether from a book dealing with the cookery of the Périgord and the Quercy. The following recipe is typical of the region, more of an *haute cuisine* creation than the better known recipes for truffles cooked in white wine, or wrapped in bacon and cooked under the embers of the fire.

LES TRUFFES EN COFFRET QUERCYNOISES
Truffles Baked in Pastry with Madeira and Foie Gras

6 fine round truffles, about 2oz each
  a *mirepoix* of finely sliced carrots, onions, celery and ham
$\frac{1}{4}$ pint Madeira
6 squares puff pastry
6 thin slices cooked ham
  a mousse of foie gras well flavoured with Madeira
1 egg yolk

Serves 6

Peel the truffles finely and braise them in Madeira with the *mirepoix*. Spread a layer of the mousse, one centimetre thick, on each slice of ham, and wrap the ham round the truffles. Put one of these little packets on each square of pastry, draw up the four corners and pinch the pastry together in the middle. Brush them over with the beaten egg yolk. Put in a fairly hot oven, Gas 5—375°F, for 20 minutes. Serve with Madeira sauce made

The goose market

from the original braising juices with the truffle peelings mixed in.

PATES, SAUSAGES AND HAMS

It is not only France which makes pâtés out of goose livers or serves up the whole liver cooked in various ways. But it is true to say that the best foie gras and goose liver pâtés come from France, where the livers attain their size and succulence through

155

the forced feeding on boiled maize. In the south-west, two varieties are used for this process: the so-called 'white' maize which is fed to the geese in the Landes below Bordeaux, and the darker reddish yellow variety which is grown in the Périgord and the Quercy. These two types of maize influence both the colour and flavour of the liver; in the Quercy and the Périgord it is a deeper rose pink and stronger in flavour, and the fat which exudes from it in the cooking is yellow, whereas it is pale cream in the Landes.

Although the specially enlarged goose and duck livers are unobtainable outside France, no book dealing with the cookery of the south-west region can omit the recipe for foie gras. I also give the recipe for pâté de foie d'oie de Périgord, as quite a respectable pâté can be made out of the livers of non-fattened geese.

BLOC FOIE GRAS
Pâté Made from the Whole Goose or Duck Liver

      1 goose or duck liver
         several slices of pork back fat for lining
         the terrine
      1 tablespoonful brandy
      1 truffle (optional)
         flour and water paste
         salt and pepper

Serves 4 to 6

Soak the liver, which will probably weigh between $1\frac{1}{2}$ to 3 pounds, for a few hours in cold water with a little salt. Trim it so that it fits comfortably into a terrine with little room to spare and pare off any discoloured parts. If you are using a truffle, scrub it with a stiff brush under running water so that it is free from mud and grit and dry it very well. Do not peel it. Line the terrine with the slices of pork fat, letting them hang down over the outside of the terrine. Cut the truffle into fine slices and insert them into the liver here and there, reserving four slices. Place two of these on the pork fat and put the liver on top. Trickle the brandy over it, season with salt and a very little pepper and put the remaining two truffle slices on top of the liver. Cover with the overhanging slices of pork fat and over the fat put a sheet of foil cut to fit the terrine.

Put the lid on the terrine and seal with a flour and water paste. Stand the terrine in a shallow pan of hot water and bake in a slow oven, Gas 1—290°F, for $2\frac{1}{2}$ to 3 hours according to the depth of the terrine. Leave the foie gras to ripen for two days in a cold place before eating.

PATE DE FOIE D'OIE
Goose Liver and Pork Pâté

1 goose liver
  its weight in finely minced pork
  slices of pork back fat for lining the terrine
  a pinch each of thyme and quatre épices
  salt and pepper
1 tablespoonful brandy

Serves 4 to 6

Soak the liver for an hour in slightly salted water. Dry it and trim off any discoloured parts. Line a small terrine with the pork fat slices, letting them hang over the edges. Season the pork with the salt and pepper, thyme and spice. Place a layer of this on the pork fat, then the liver. Trickle the brandy over it and cover with the rest of the pork and then the overhanging back fat slices. Cover with a piece of tin foil and then the lid of the terrine. Cook in a shallow pan of water in a low oven, Gas 1—290°F, for 1 to 1½ hours depending on the depth of the terrine. Ripen in a cold place for two days before eating.

FOIE GRAS FRAIS AUX CAPRES
Fresh Foie Gras with Capers

Recipe from Monsieur Escorbiac

1 large duck or goose liver, about 1½ to 2lb
½ pint white wine
   small glass Madeira
   thyme and a bayleaf
   sauce velouté
6 tablespoonfuls cream
   few drops lemon juice
4 tablespoonfuls capers

Serves 4 to 6

Although it is not possible for cooks outside France to produce dishes such as this, I am including this recipe and the following one as examples of typical local variations in methods of dealing with geese and duck livers. This recipe comes from Monsieur Escorbiac of Cahors, capital of the Quercy, where it is a speciality.

Poach the liver in white wine (not too dry) to which you have added a small glass of Madeira, thyme and a bayleaf. Leave the liver to cool in the liquid. Next day, remove the fat which will have exuded from the liver and strain the liquid. Cut the liver into escalops. Add the same amount of *sauce velouté* to the liquid and finish off with 6 tablespoonfuls of cream, a few drops of lemon juice and 4 tablespoonfuls of capers. Pour over the slices of liver.

LE FOIE AUX RAISINS
Goose or Duck Liver with Grapes

1 large duck or goose liver weighing
  approximately 1½ to 2lbs
½ lb white grapes
¼ pint white wine
4 shallots

Serves 4 to 6

Wrap the cleaned and soaked liver in buttered greaseproof
paper and put into a hot oven, Gas 6—400°F, for 15 minutes.
Unwrap the liver, add the peeled and pipped grapes, the white
wine, a very little water and the shallots and cook for another
20 minutes in a moderate oven, Gas 4—355°F, basting the liver
with the juices in the pan. Serve the liver in slices with the
grapes arranged around and the strained sauce, skimmed of its
fat, poured over. If you wish to serve the liver cold, leave it to
cool in the juices overnight so that the fat will be easier to take
off.

PATE DE FOIE DE COCHON
Pork Liver Pâté

1 lb pig's liver
2 lb pork taken from the neck
1 onion
1 tablespoonful brandy
1 pinch quatre épices
1 clove garlic
  salt and pepper
1 bayleaf

159

1 piece of pig's caul about a foot square
2 oz pure pork fat
½ glass white wine
1 carrot
1 leek

Serves 4 to 6

Mince the meat and liver together, putting them through the finest blade of the mincer. Add the finely chopped onion and garlic, the bayleaf, spice, salt and pepper. Pour the brandy over and leave in a cool place for 24 hours. Soak the caul in water if it is stiff, spread it out and put the mixture in the centre. Draw up the edges together and tie with string. Melt the fat in a heavy pan, brown the pâté all over, add the white wine and the sliced carrot and leek, and braise it gently for 2 hours. Remove it carefully and put it into a terrine where it will just fit comfortably. Strain the juices over it. If it is not completely covered, add a little more melted pork fat. When the fat has set, cover with a piece of tin foil and the lid of the terrine. Leave for two or three days before eating.

PATE CHAUD DE PIGEONNAUX DE PERIGORD
Hot Pigeon Pâté

5 pigeons
½ lb minced pork
½ lb minced veal
¼ lb minced fresh pork fat
1 large or 2 small eggs
1 clove garlic
2 shallots

160

2 truffles (optional)
grated peel of a small lemon
a pinch of quatre épices or nutmeg
1 crushed bayleaf
1 teaspoonful very finely chopped parsley
¼ teaspoonful thyme
2 tablespoonfuls cognac
1 oz butter
salt and pepper
1½ lb puff or flaky pastry
1 egg yolk beaten up with a dessertspoonful
water
½ pint sauce Périgueux

Serves 6

Cut off the breasts from four pigeons, skin them, flatten them
with a cutlet bat and marinate them in the cognac for 2 hours.
If you are using truffles, put them to marinate with the pigeon
breasts. Bone the fifth pigeon and cut off the remaining flesh
from the others. Mince all this finely and add to the other
minced meats. Pound them in a mortar or blend in an electric
blender for 2 minutes. Soften the sliced shallots in the butter
and put them in a bowl. Add the meat mixture, the crushed
garlic, the seasonings and the marinating juices from the pigeon
breasts. Beat in the egg and continue beating the mixture hard
with a wooden spoon for a few minutes. Spread a thin layer on
each of the breast fillets, put a small piece of truffle, if you are
using it, in the centre and roll them up.

Butter a 2½ pint hinged metal mould and line with the
pastry, keeping enough back for the lid. Put half the stuffing in
and then arrange the rolled breast fillets neatly over it. Cover
with the rest of the stuffing and with the pastry lid. Make a
small hole in the centre and insert a small foil or brown paper

L

funnel so that the steam escapes in the cooking. Knock up the edges of the pastry and decorate with pastry leaves and roses. Brush over with the rest of the egg yolk and water and put into a hot oven, Gas 6—400°F, for 15 minutes, then turn down the heat to Gas 4—355°F and continue baking for 1¼ hours, protecting the lid with foil or brown paper if it browns too much. Leave to cool for 10 to 15 minutes before taking it out of the mould. Lift off the lid carefully and put in four spoonfuls of the sauce Périgueux. Replace the lid and return to the oven at the same temperature for 8 to 10 minutes to firm up the sides. Serve hot with the rest of the sauce. It is also good cold.

CONFIT D'OIE OU DE CANARD
Goose or Duck Preserved in its Own Fat

As you walk through the markets in the winter, you will often see stalls selling geese and ducks with their carcases removed but with the wing and leg bones left in the meat. These are called *paletots* and are the birds prepared for the confits, which can be made in two ways. The traditional method preserves the birds in stoneware jars under a layer of their own fat. The jars are stored in a cool, dark, dry larder, their contents being reheated in May to prevent the fat from going rancid. The other more modern method is to preserve the birds in glass jars under sterilisation. Prepared in this way, they have the advantage of keeping almost indefinitely and do not need reheating, but the flavour is not nearly so fine.

Confit Prepared in Stoneware Jars

In addition to the poultry you will need:
cooking salt

black pepper
ground cloves
bayleaves
thyme
saltpetre
pure pork fat if there is not enough
from the birds

You can either joint the birds and make the confits without boning them, or take out the carcase, as is more usual. If your butcher or poultry dealer will not do this the procedure is as follows. First cut off the neck and wing tips, and the feet at the knee-joint. Open the bird by cutting right down the back. Keeping the blade of the knife turned inwards towards the bone, scrape and cut away the meat from the carcase. Sever it at the wing and leg-joints.

Cut the boned bird into four pieces. Rub the pieces all over with salt to which you have added a teaspoonful of thyme, a crushed bayleaf, half a teaspoonful each of ground cloves, freshly milled black pepper and a good pinch of salt petre for every $4\frac{1}{2}$ pounds of meat. Leave for 24 hours, and then wipe them. Cut off as much of the fat as possible without damaging the meat and melt it slowly in a heavy cast-iron pan. Add the pieces of meat and, if there is not enough fat to cover them, add pure pork fat. Simmer very slowly for 2 to $2\frac{1}{2}$ hours, by which time the meat should be very tender and, when it is pierced with a fine skewer or knitting needle, the juices should run pale yellow.

Remove the meat with a slotted spoon and put into a large stoneware jar which has previously been well scrubbed out with boiling soda-water and sterilised. Continue cooking the fat in the cast-iron pan for a further 10 to 15 minutes. Strain it over the pieces of confit and make sure that there are at least 2 inches of fat covering the pieces of meat. Leave to get quite cold and

163

then cover with a double thickness of tin foil. Store in a cool, dry larder.

Confit in Sterilised Glass Jars

Same ingredients as on page 162

Prepare the meat in the same way as in the preceding recipe but do not cut off the fat. Leave, rubbed with the salt, herbs and spices, for 24 hours and then put the pieces to cook very gently in a heavy cast-iron pan. When the pieces of meat are half cooked put them into well washed and sterilised large glass jars. The best jars for this purpose are the French preserving jars with wide necks and clip down lids, which are obtainable in Britain. Allow three or four pieces per jar, pushing them well down, for they will shrink in the final cooking. Add a sprig of fresh thyme and a dessertspoonful of brandy for each jar and pour in enough of the fat to come halfway up.

Seal the jars, wrap them in newspaper and then a cloth and put them in the largest pan or cauldron you have. Place weights on top of the jars to stop them moving about, and cover with water. Bring very slowly to the boil (this should take about $1\frac{1}{2}$ hours) and boil for 3 hours, topping up with boiling water to cover the jars whenever necessary. Do not cool in the water, but remove as soon as possible after the end of the cooking time. Wipe down and store in a dry larder.

LE COU D'OIE FARCI
Stuffed Goose Neck

This is made and cooked together with the confits of goose and duck.

1 goose neck
1 lb fresh minced pork
2 chicken or duck livers
1 truffle (if possible)
2 tablespoonfuls brandy
   salt and pepper

Serves 4

Turn the goose neck skin inside out, being very careful not to tear it. Marinate it in the brandy for 12 hours or overnight. Clean the truffle and chop it finely with the chicken or duck livers. Mix with the pork and the brandy from the marinade, and season with salt and pepper. Stuff the neck, sew it up at both ends and put it to cook in the fat with the pieces of goose for 2½ hours.

This can be eaten either cold, cut in slices, or hot, in which case it is fried for a few minutes in some of its own fat. It can also be added to a cassoulet, like the stuffed duck neck which is made in exactly the same way.

LES GRILLONS DE PERIGORD
Potted Pork

Grillons for the Périgourdins is another name for *rillettes* except that the pieces of meat are sometimes a little larger than the finely shredded mixture one buys in the shops at Le Mans and Tours, two areas in France with well justified reputations for their rillettes. Enormous quantities of grillons are made in the winter in the Périgord and then stored in the larder, to be taken out when needed and eaten for hors d'oeuvres, spread on bread for the afternoon snack (known as *Les Quatre Heures* and taking place any time between four and six o'clock) or put into stuffings for vegetables and eggs.

2 lb lean pork from the neck, shoulder,
  lean belly or lean spare rib
2 lb back fat
$2\frac{1}{2}$ oz cooking salt
2 shallots
2 cloves garlic
2 or 3 sprigs each of thyme and parsley
2 crushed bayleaves
$\frac{1}{2}$ teaspoonful freshly ground black pepper
$\frac{1}{2}$ teaspoonful quatre épices or mixed spice
5 fluid oz dry white wine
  Extra pure pork fat if necessary

Chop the meat as finely as possible, put it in a bowl with the salt, pepper, bayleaves and spice and leave overnight. Next day, put it with the parsley, thyme and white wine in a very heavy casserole and simmer, covered, over a very low flame for 6 hours. The liquid and melted fat should barely shudder. Stir every so often to prevent it from sticking. After 4 hours, add the very finely chopped shallots and crushed garlic.

Put the mixture into a sieve, colander or wire mesh basket over a bowl so that the fat and juices are strained off, and then shred and chop it a little finer. Do not put it through the mincer, either before or after you cook the meat, but if you have an electric blender the final chopping can be speeded up by putting small amounts at a time into the machine and giving it one very quick whirl, just enough to break down the meat a little more without reducing it to a porridge. Taste the mixture to see if there is enough salt—it should be well seasoned—and then put it into sterilised glass jars, terrines or stoneware pots. Take off the fat when it has set in the bowl, melt it down and strain over the grillons. They should be covered by half an inch of fat, so if there is not enough, add more pork fat. When it has set, tie a double thickness of greaseproof paper or foil over the pots and store in a cool dry larder. The grillons will keep for several months.

LES GRILLONS D'OIE
Potted Goose

These used to be made from all the debris left at the bottom of the pot in which the confits had been cooked. Nowadays they are made from fresh birds. To cut up a whole goose for grillons is rather an expensive procedure, but if you want to use only half a goose for another dish (such as a stew with haricot beans) the other half can be potted and preserved for several months as a standby for hors d'oeuvres.

$\frac{1}{2}$ a goose, boned
  its weight in back fat, or fat belly of pork
2 shallots
2 cloves garlic
$\frac{1}{2}$ teaspoonful quatre épices or mixed spice
  a large pinch of thyme
1 crushed bayleaf

Cut the meat and fat into very small pieces or strips and put them in a heavy casserole. Season with salt and pepper and put to simmer for 1 hour on a very low flame with a little water (about $\frac{1}{4}$ pint for 4 lb of meat and fat), by which time some of the fat will have melted. Stir frequently with a wooden spoon to prevent it from sticking. Chop the garlic and shallots finely and add to the casserole with the thyme, bayleaf and spice. Transfer to a very low oven, Gas 1—290°F, for 4 hours. Strain through a wire sieve and taste for seasoning.

Shred and pound the **meat** finely, or put into the electric blender, giving the machine two or three quick whirls, just enough to break down the fibres without reducing the meat to one homogenous mass. Put into sterilised glass jars or stoneware pots. Take off the fat which has set in the bowl, melt it down and strain over the goose. Cover, when cool, with a double thickness of greaseproof paper or foil and store in a cool dry larder. Keep the grillons out of the refrigerator at all times if possible; the texture should be soft so that they can easily be spread on bread.

Duck, turkey and rabbit can be treated successfully in the same way.

LA SANGUETTE

After the geese and ducks have been fattened for three weeks on their diet of boiled maize, they are then killed, plucked and singed, wiped down with a cloth and hung up by their necks in a cool airy spot ready to be taken to market and sold. If she has many to pluck, the farmer's wife will invite the neighbouring wives to lend a hand and they will all sit round in a circle, chattering in patois over their work and throwing the feathers into large sacks standing in the centre, which will then be sold as stuffing for pillows and mattresses.

Sometimes it happens that the skin of the birds gets torn in the plucking or through oversingeing, in which case their necks are slit and they are hung up by their feet over a large dish so that the blood which drips down is not wasted. This blood is then mixed with a little salt, pepper and garlic and left to coagulate, after which it is either fried in a little oil with onions and parsley or, as is more usual, cooked first in a casserole with a little salt water for about 15 minutes until it resembles a round, rust-coloured cake. It is then drained, cut into slices and cooked slowly in a little goose fat with onions, parsley and more garlic.

It has a curious flavour and texture, and one's taste for it is definitely an acquired one, but I have included this description as the recipe is a purely regional one from the Périgord and something of a curiosity.

BALLOTTINES
Preserved Fillets

These are fillets of poultry, game or pork, or the whole birds boned and stuffed, and then preserved in glass jars in a stock which when cold sets to a light jelly.

Ballottine of Guineafowl

  1 guineafowl
  $\frac{3}{4}$ lb minced pork
  1 split calf's foot or pig's trotter
  2 carrots
  1 stick of celery
  1 onion stuck with a clove
  1 clove garlic
   a bouquet garni
  2 eggs
   a pinch each of thyme and quatre épices
  1 bayleaf
   salt and pepper
  1 glass of white wine, about 5 fluid oz
  2 tablespoonfuls of brandy
  1 oz pork, duck or chicken dripping

  Serves 4

Bone the bird by cutting down the back with a sharp knife and gently working your way down the side of the carcase, taking care always to keep the blade of the knife towards the bone.

169

Sever the wing and leg bones at the joints and gently ease them out with the sinews. Cut off the neck at the joint by the carcase. Be very careful not to pierce the skin anywhere. Lay the bird out flat on a board and carefully cut out the fillets on each side of the breast. Divide them into two longwise so that you now have four fillets. Season the bird with salt and pepper, moisten with a few drops of brandy, roll it up in a clean cloth and set aside in a cool place while preparing the stock and stuffing.

Slice the vegetables thinly and let them melt in a pan with the dripping. Add half the white wine and let this bubble for a few minutes. Add the carcase and the bones, the giblets (but not the liver) and the calf's foot or pig's trotter, which should be well scrubbed and split. Cover with water, bring to the boil, skim and add the bouquet garni, salt and pepper. Simmer for 3 hours, adding the rest of the white wine after $1\frac{1}{2}$ hours. Strain and when quite cold remove all the fat. Clarify the stock in a clean pan with the slightly beaten whites of 2 eggs, and strain carefully through a muslin lined strainer.

Mince the pork and the liver of the bird finely together. Add the salt and pepper, thyme, quatre épices and brandy. Sew up the holes where you cut out the leg and wing bones and put some of the stuffing in the pockets. Lay the bird out flat on a clean board and put a layer of the stuffing on it. On top place two of the fillets, seasoned with more salt and pepper, then another layer of the stuffing, the other two fillets, also seasoned, and a final layer of stuffing. Gather up the edges of the bird and sew it up so that it resembles a sausage and put it in a large sterilised glass preserving jar. Melt down the stock, which should have set to a light jelly, and pour it over the bird so that it comes halfway up the jar. Seal the jar, wrap it in newspaper and then a cloth and put it upright in a tall pan with a weight on it. Cover with water, bring very slowly to the boil, allowing between 1 and $1\frac{1}{2}$ hours for the water to reach boiling point, and then boil for 3 hours, taking care to see that the jar is covered at all times with boiling water. Do not allow it to cool in the water.

Ballottine of Turkey

This is preserved in the same way as the ballottine of guinea-fowl, but only the fillets from the breast are used. They may either be preserved plain in the stock, or flattened out, stuffed, rolled up and fastened with toothpicks. They will need 1½ hours' boiling.

JAMBON DE PAYS
Local Method of Curing Hams

Recipe from the Auberge du Moulin de Guiral,
St Martin de Redon

Dry the ham and rub it all over with ground black pepper. Cut a piece of linen or muslin 2½ times the size of the ham. Rub the ham all over with *gros sel* (sea salt), paying special attention to the area round the bone and pressing it well in all over. Put a layer of the salt ¼ inch thick on the linen and place the ham flesh side down so that it is in contact with the salt. Scatter another layer of salt over the top (the rind side) and fold the linen over, enclosing the ham completely. Tie round with string to secure it, and then wrap it up in brown paper.

Fill a wooden crate or tub with sifted wood ash and put the ham in it with weights on the top. The ash should completely cover the ham. Cover with a wooden lid and leave in a dry place for one month. Then unwrap the ham and brush off all the salt. Rub the ham all over with pure white spirit or brandy (in the Périgord and the Quercy eau-de-vie is used). Have ready a muslin or linen bag large enough to fit the ham and envelop it in the bag. Tie the end of the bag round the bone with twine or string and hang to dry in a cool, dry, airy larder or barn for 3 months.

FISH

CARPE FARCIE EN CROUTE
Stuffed Carp in Pastry

1 carp, 3-4 lbs
$\frac{1}{4}$ lb minced fresh pork or veal
$\frac{1}{4}$ lb minced ham
$\frac{1}{4}$ lb mushrooms
  parsley, thyme and tarragon
2 onions
1 clove garlic
1 egg
2 carrots
2 tablespoonfuls oil
6 fluid oz white wine
1 dessertspoonful cognac
$\frac{3}{4}$ lb puff pastry

Serves 4 to 6

Have the carp cleaned and scaled by the fishmonger, but leave the head on. Make a stuffing with the pork or veal and ham, one onion, the garlic and the egg. Season it with the herbs, salt and pepper and add the cognac. Stuff the fish with it and fasten with toothpicks or sew it up. Slice the other onion and the carrots thinly and put them in a roasting dish. Put the carp on top and pour the oil and wine over it. Bake in a moderate oven, Gas 5—375°F, for 1 hour, basting with the juices.

Remove the fish to an ovenproof dish into which it will fit comfortably with not too much room on either side. Skim off the excess fat from the juices and put the sauce, onions and carrots through a sieve. Correct the seasoning if necessary and pour the sauce over the fish. Cover with the pastry and brush over with milk. Bake in a fairly hot oven, Gas 6—400°F, for 30 minutes.

FILETS DE SOLE BRANTOMOISES
Stuffed Fillets of Sole

2 soles
$\frac{1}{4}$ lb minced veal
1 small cod steak
1 egg yolk
1 dessertspoonful breadcrumbs, soaked in a
   little milk and squeezed dry
1 dessertspoonful parsley
$\frac{1}{2}$ lb mushrooms
3 oz butter
2 dessertspoonfuls flour
   juice of half a lemon
1 onion
   half a glass of white wine

Serves 4

Ask the fishmonger to fillet each sole into four and to give you the bones and trimmings. Make a court bouillon with the trimmings, the onion, the white wine and $1\frac{1}{2}$ pints of water. Season with salt, pepper and the bouquet garni, bring to the boil and simmer for 20 minutes. Add the cod steak and poach it gently in the liquid for 10 minutes. Drain, reserving the liquid, and flake the cod finely. Mix it with the veal, parsley, breadcrumbs and egg yolk. Season with salt and pepper and put a little of this stuffing on each of the fillets. Roll them up and put them in a fireproof dish. Pour $\frac{1}{2}$ pint of the fish stock over them and add $1\frac{1}{2}$ oz of the butter, salt and pepper. Bake, basting with the juices, in a moderate oven, Gas 4—355°F, for 30 minutes.

173

Meanwhile sweat the quartered mushrooms for a few minutes in ½oz butter, the juice of half a lemon and 2 tablespoonfuls water. Drain. When the fish is cooked, drain off and reserve the juices. Melt the rest of the butter in a small pan, add the flour gradually and simmer for about 1 minute until the roux is pale gold in colour. Add the juices from the fish and enough of the reserved fish stock to make a smooth sauce, not too thin. Add the mushrooms, correct the seasoning and pour over the fish. Return to the oven for 5 minutes; serve garnished with parsley.

In the old days, when truffles were far more plentiful, the recipe included two, half of one sliced and added to the stuffing and the rest chopped and added to the sauce with the mushrooms.

FILETS DE SOLE DE PERIGORD
Stuffed Fillets of Sole with Ham and Mushrooms

8 sole fillets
½ lb mushrooms, the small flat variety if possible
2 tablespoonfuls finely chopped spring onions
1 finely chopped clove garlic
1 finely diced thin slice of ham
1 tablespoonful finely chopped parsley
¾ pint fish stock made with the fish trimmings, 1 onion, 6 peppercorns and a bouquet garni
¾ pint white wine
4 tablespoonfuls butter
3 tablespoonfuls oil
1½ oz flour

Fish Farce

½ lb skinned and boned minced whiting
¼ lb mushroom stalks

174

1 finely chopped shallot
1 egg white
6 tablespoonfuls double cream
1 tablespoonful butter
1 tablespoonful oil
  a few drops of lemon juice

Serves 4

Make the farce first. Sauté the finely chopped mushroom stalks and shallot in the butter and oil with the lemon juice until they have softened. Turn up the heat and cook fiercely until the mixture is dry. Cool and add to the minced whiting. Beat the egg white until it is foamy and whisk into the mushrooms and fish. Put the mixture through a sieve and beat in half the cream. Season with salt and pepper and beat in the rest of the cream. Place a small spoonful of the stuffing on each of the fillets, roll them up and fasten with toothpicks or tie round with cotton. Make a brown roux with the butter and flour and gradually add ½ pint each of the wine and fish stock, stirring until you have a smooth sauce. Season with salt and pepper and simmer, partially covered, for 30 minutes, stirring occasionally.

Put the fish fillets in a buttered fireproof dish. Scatter the chopped spring onions over them, moisten with the rest of the wine and stock and cover with a piece of buttered paper. Bake in a moderate oven, Gas 4—355°F, for 20 minutes. Meanwhile, sauté the mushrooms, garlic and ham together in the oil for 10 minutes. Stir in the parsley.

Drain off the cooking liquid from the fish fillets and boil it down until it has reached a syrupy consistency. Add to the sauce. Put the fillets in a circle on a heated dish with the mushrooms and ham in the centre. Spoon the sauce over them and glaze under a grill for 1 minute.

MOULES A L'OSEILLE
Mussels with Sorrel

3 quarts cleaned mussels
1 tablespoonful oil
3 large glasses dry white wine
2 tablespoonfuls chopped parsley
3 cloves garlic
2 oz mild gammon

Serves 4 to 6

Put the mussels to open in a wide pan with the white wine and cook rapidly. Remove as soon as they are opened and shell them. Dice the gammon as finely as possible and chop the garlic. Heat the oil in a pan and sauté the mussels, together with the garlic, gammon and parsley, for 3 or 4 minutes. Serve on a bed of *fondu d'oseille* with triangles of fried bread arranged round the dish.

MEAT AND POULTRY

LE JAMBON CONFIT
Grilled Gammon with Onions

1 mild gammon steak per person
1 small onion per person
1 dessertspoonful vinegar per person
black pepper

Grill the gammon steaks slowly on both sides until they are almost but not quite cooked through. They should still be soft. Meanwhile chop the onion as finely as possible until it is almost a purée. Mix with the vinegar and season with black pepper.

Spread it on the gammon, put the steaks on a flat serving dish and cover with a plate. Place over a pan of gently boiling water and leave for 10 minutes. Serve immediately.

In the country, where every farmhouse still has a large fireplace, this is made with the locally cured ham, grilled over the fire and then put to rest on top of the big cast-iron pots standing on the hearth.

PAUPIETTES DE VEAU PERIGOURDINE
Stuffed Escalops of Veal

8 small veal escalops
2 pieces of preserved duck or goose
1 slice bread
3 shallots
1 clove garlic
1 egg
1 tablespoonful chopped parsley
  salt, pepper and a pinch of nutmeg
2 carrots
1 onion
2 oz unsmoked bacon
2 oz dried mushrooms
½ oz flour
⅓ pint sweet white wine

Serves 4

Beat the escalops out thin. Scrape off the fat from the pieces of preserved duck or goose and bone them. Chop finely and mix with the chopped shallots, garlic, parsley, egg and bread, previously soaked in a little water and then squeezed so that the excess moisture is removed. Season with salt, pepper and the nutmeg. Put a little of the stuffing on each of the escalops, roll them up, tucking them in at both ends so that none of the stuffing escapes, and tie them round with string or cotton. Soak the mushrooms in warm water. Slice the onion and the carrots. Take the fat which you scraped off from the pieces of preserved poultry and melt it in a heavy pan. You will need a good two tablespoonfuls, and if you find there is not enough, add a little more from the jar of confit or a little pork fat. Soften the onions and carrots in it and then brown the paupiettes carefully on all sides, together with the diced bacon. Remove with a slotted spoon to a dish and keep warm.

Sprinkle the flour over the fat in the pan, let it simmer for a few minutes until it is a warm gold in colour and then add the wine gradually, stirring until you have a smooth sauce. Add two tablespoonfuls of the water in which the mushrooms are soaking, put back the meat, cover and braise very gently for 1 hour. Add the soaked mushrooms, drained, together with a little more of their liquid, season with salt and pepper and braise again for 1 more hour. Serve the escalops on a hot dish with the sauce and mushrooms poured over.

L'ESTOUFFAT A L'AGENAISE
Beef Stew with Prunes

2 lb stewing beef
a marinade (see page 199)
1 lb prunes
½ pint beef stock
1 tablespoonful flour
1 oz dripping

Serves 4 to 6

Soak the prunes and cut the beef into pieces. Marinate the beef in the marinade for 48 hours. Strain, reserving the marinade, wipe the pieces dry with kitchen paper or a cloth and brown in the fat. Pour over the marinade including the vegetables, cover and cook very slowly in a slow oven, Gas 2—310°F, for 2½ hours. Meanwhile simmer the stoned and soaked prunes in a little salted water. Remove the meat to a dish together with the prunes and keep warm. Reduce the liquid in which the meat has cooked by fast boiling. Mix the flour and the stock to a paste in a bowl and add to the sauce, and then put it, together with the vegetables, through a sieve. Add to the meat and prunes and simmer very gently on top of the stove for another 15 minutes.

RAGOUT DE BOEUF AUX CAPRES
Beef Stew with Capers

2 lb stewing beef
½ lb leeks
1 lb onions
4 carrots
1 pint red wine
2 cloves garlic
1 oz butter
2 tablespoonfuls oil
2 cloves
   a large pinch each of nutmeg and cinnamon
1 sugar lump
1 oz flour
4 dessertspoonfuls capers
   a bouquet garni

Serves 4 to 6

Soften the cleaned and finely sliced vegetables in the butter and oil and remove with a slotted spoon to a heavy cocotte or an earthenware casserole. Brown the meat carefully all over in the fat remaining in the pan and add to the vegetables. Sprinkle the flour into the remaining juices and cook slowly, stirring continuously until you have a brown roux. Add the wine, previously brought to the boil in a small pan and set alight, and stir over the heat until the sauce is smooth. Pour it over the meat and vegetables, add the sugar lump, spices and herbs and season with salt and pepper. Cover and transfer to a very low oven, Gas 1—290°F, for 3 hours. Then add 3 dessertspoonfuls of capers and cook for 1 more hour. Thicken the sauce with a beurre manié made by working together $\frac{1}{2}$ oz of butter with $\frac{1}{2}$ oz of flour and adding it slowly to the stew, and finally add the last dessertspoonful of capers. Heat through to almost boiling point and serve with plain boiled potatoes.

EPAULE D'AGNEAU EN COCOTTE
Braised Shoulder of Lamb

1 boned shoulder of lamb
2 cloves garlic
4 rashers unsmoked streaky bacon
4 onions
4 carrots
a bouquet garni
6 cloves
$\frac{1}{2}$ teaspoonful nutmeg
$\frac{3}{4}$ pint meat stock
1 egg yolk

Serves 4 to 6

Make small incisions all over the meat and insert small slivers of garlic and bacon (reserving two of the slices). Roll up the meat and tie it round with string or fine twine. Put in a cocotte with the onions and carrots, peeled and sliced, the herbs, spices, salt, pepper and the bone. Place the other two slices of bacon on top, pour the stock over and boil fiercely for 5 minutes. Cover the cocotte, lower the heat and braise slowly for 1½ hours.

Remove to a serving dish and keep warm. Skim off the excess fat, add the egg yolk and thicken the sauce. Serve very hot, accompanied by a dish of cabbage braised with chestnuts and small onions in a little fat and stock.

LA FRICASSEE DE COCHON
Pork Stewed in White Wine

2 lb boned shoulder or neck of pork, cut into
   medium sized cubes
1 lb carrots, sliced
¾ lb onions, sliced
   just under 1½ pints dry white wine
4 shallots
2 oz pork fat
½ teaspoonful nutmeg
   salt and pepper
1 tablespoonful cornflour
1 lump sugar

Serves 4 to 6

Fry the meat in half the fat in a heavy cast-iron cocotte. In another pan, fry the onions and carrots in the rest of the fat until the onions are softened and translucent. Heat the wine, set it alight and add it to the meat with the carrots and onions. It should just cover the meat. Add the chopped shallots and the nutmeg, and season with salt and pepper. Cook for 3 hours with the lid on the pan on top of the stove and with an asbestos mat underneath. The liquid should just shudder, not boil. Leave until the next day.

Cook again very slowly for another 2 hours. Thicken with the cornflour mixed to a smooth paste with a little water, taste for

seasoning and add the lump of sugar. Stir until the sugar is
dissolved and serve with slices of French bread which you have
toasted and rubbed on both sides with a clove of cut garlic.

L'ALICOT DES ABATIS
Goose or Turkey Giblet Stew

In the geese and duck markets of south-west France, the
giblets and wingtips of the birds which have been boned for the
confits are sold tied up in little cellophane packets, ready to be
taken home and stewed with salt pork and vegetables. The stew
can be made with turkey or goose giblets, but if you want to
make it with the giblets from a duck, you will need two sets or
you will have to augment the one set with a chicken's giblets.
Whichever you are using, the rest of the ingredients are the
same.

> giblets as described above
> $\frac{1}{2}$ lb salt pork or gammon
> $\frac{1}{2}$ lb haricot beans
> 2 carrots
> 2 onions
> 1 small celeriac
> 2 or 3 cloves garlic
> 2 tablespoonfuls goose, duck, turkey or pork fat
> 1 oz flour
> a large bouquet garni
> salt and pepper

Serves 4 to 6

Soak the beans overnight and then put them on to cook,
covered with fresh water and salt. Boil gently for 30 minutes and
then add the giblets (but not the liver), the wingtips and, if
possible, the feet of the bird. Simmer for 1 hour. Melt the fat in

a casserole and brown the salt pork or gammon, cut into chunks, the sliced onions and carrots, the garlic and the celeriac, cut into squares of about 1½ inches. Remove with a slotted spoon and add the flour to make a roux. Put back the vegetables, add the giblets and wingtips, but not the feet, and the beans. Add enough of the stock so that the meat and vegetables are barely covered, season with salt and pepper and add the herbs. Cover and simmer very gently for 1 hour.

LE CASSOULET PERIGOURDIN
Beans with Mutton, Sausage and Stuffed Goose Neck

In *L'Art du Bien Manger* Edmond Richardin lists several cassoulets, but wherever you go in south-west France, practically every department or town has its own version. This is the variation worked out for Richardin by Fulbert Dumonteil, the gastronomic writer from the Périgord.

1½ lb haricot beans
4 onions
4 or 5 cloves garlic
1 lb boned leg or shoulder of mutton
1 lb coarse cut garlic sausage, of the type
known as Toulouse sausage
1 stuffed duck or goose neck, truffled if
possible
¼ lb unsmoked fat bacon
5 tablespoonfuls goose fat
1½ pints meat stock
3 dessertspoonfuls tomato purée
a large bouquet garni
1½ oz breadcrumbs
2 tablespoonfuls chopped parsley

Serves 8

183

Soak the beans overnight. **Drain them, put** them into a large pan and cover them with fresh water. Add salt and pepper, one onion, a clove of garlic and the bouquet garni and boil gently for 1½ hours. Melt the goose fat in a large casserole. Put in the mutton (cut into chunks), the sausage (cut into slices) and pieces of preserved goose neck. Fry them gently in the fat for about 10 minutes; then in a separate pan fry the finely sliced onion and garlic with the diced bacon. Cover the meats with the drained beans and scatter the onion, garlic and bacon over the top. Add the stock in which you have dissolved the tomato purée, season with salt and pepper and cook in a very low oven, Gas 1/2—290°/310°F, for 3 hours. Scatter the breadcrumbs mixed with the parsley over the casserole contents, turn up the oven to Gas 3—335°F and continue cooking for about 20 minutes until the crumbs have formed a golden crust.

Some people may prefer to roast the mutton partially first in a gentle oven, adding the sausage halfway through the cooking time. In this case the cassoulet need be cooked for only 2½ hours before the breadcrumbs are added.

The *cassoulet Quercynoise* differs from that of the Périgord in including neither the neck nor the mutton, and replacing them with confit de porc and smoked sausages.

L'OIE A LA MIE
Roast Goose

This is a very well-known dish in the Périgord and the Quercy. Some cooks like first to simmer the bird in stock made from the giblets with onions, leeks and carrots before covering it with breadcrumbs and browning it in the oven. Others, including the lady who gave me the recipe, roast the bird, as follows.

1 young goose
½ lb minced pork

    2 shallots
    8 tablespoonfuls fresh white breadcrumbs
    1 clove garlic
    ¼ lb mushrooms
      a little parsley
    1 egg
      a pinch of nutmeg
    2 tablespoonfuls cognac
    4 tablespoonfuls gherkins

    Serves 6 to 8

Chop the liver of the goose with the shallots, parsley, garlic and mushrooms. Mix with two tablespoonfuls of the breadcrumbs and the pork and bind with the egg. Stir in the cognac, add the nutmeg and season with salt and pepper. Stuff the goose and roast it on a rack in a moderate oven, Gas 4—355°F, for 1 hour 50 minutes, basting every so often with a little stock made from the giblets. From time to time syphon off the fat from the tin with a bulb baster. Take the bird out of the oven and cover it all over with remaining breadcrumbs, pressing them well down. Return to the oven for another 15 to 20 minutes until the crumbs have formed a golden crust.

Serve with a gravy made from the stock and the juices from the pan, skimmed of all the fat, into which you have stirred 4 tablespoonfuls of finely chopped gherkins.

RAGOUT D'OIE AUX HARICOTS
Goose Stewed with Haricot Beans

    1 goose
    ¾ lb haricot beans
    2 onions
    2 leeks

1 lb tomatoes
3 carrots
1 clove garlic
1 bottle white wine
½ pint stock made from the giblets
2 tablespoonfuls goose fat, dripping or butter
   salt, pepper and a large bouquet garni

Serves 6 to 8

Joint the goose and turn the pieces in the fat until they are golden. Add the finely sliced onions, leeks and carrots, the previously soaked and drained haricot beans, and finally the roughly chopped tomatoes. Pour in the wine and stock, season with salt and pepper and add the bouquet garni. Cover the casserole and simmer for 2½ hours or until the pieces of goose and the beans are tender. Pour off the sauce and leave to cool. Put the casserole in the lowest possible oven while you skim off the fat. Put back the sauce in the casserole, heat through gently and serve.

COQ EN PATE
Chicken in Pastry

1 roasting chicken
¼ lb minced fresh pork
¼ lb chicken livers
2 oz mousse de foie or pâté truffé
   thyme and parsley
1 tablespoonful Madeira
   salt and pepper
12 oz puff pastry
2 tablespoonfuls butter
1 truffle if possible
1 egg yolk

Serves 4 to 6

Mix together the pork, the chopped chicken livers and the mousse de foie or pâté. Season with the herbs, salt and pepper and add the Madeira and the sliced truffle. Stuff the chicken with the mixture. Roast the chicken on its side in the butter in a hot oven for 30 minutes, turning it over after 15 minutes and basting very frequently. Cool. Wrap it in the rolled-out pastry, cut a small slit at the top to allow the steam to escape, brush with egg yolk and bake in a moderate oven, Gas 5—375°F, for 40 minutes. Serve with a Madeira sauce.

PINTADE AUX MARRONS
Guineafowl with Chestnuts

Guineafowl are reared as commonly as chickens, ducks and geese in south-west France. Their flesh can be rather dry unless carefully roasted or braised. Before they are killed a spoonful of cognac is forced down their throats and this is said to improve their flavour and tenderise them.

1 guineafowl
2 oz butter
½ pint chicken or game stock
1 lb chestnuts
1 small onion

Serves 4

Peel the chestnuts and cook them in boiling salted water until they are tender but still whole. Roast the guineafowl for 30 minutes in the butter in a moderately hot oven, Gas 5—375°F, basting frequently with half the stock and the juices in the pan. Put the chestnuts and the onion, cut into very fine rings, under the bird in the pan and continue roasting for another 30 minutes, basting every 10 minutes and adding the rest of the stock gradually. The chestnuts will have absorbed a good deal of the juices at the end, but should still be very moist.

CAKES AND SWEETS

LES GAUFRES DE PERIGORD
Aniseed Waffles

8 oz flour
6 oz caster sugar
a pinch of salt
1 dessertspoonful crushed aniseed grains
   or 1 teaspoonful aniseed water
1 tablespoonful brandy
6 eggs

Serves 4 to 6

Sift the flour and salt into a large bowl, add the sugar and make a well in the centre. Drop in the eggs, mix them in one by one and then stir in the aniseed and brandy. Beat the batter hard with a wooden spoon for at least 10 minutes, then leave to rest for 5 hours. Beat again, heat and grease the waffle iron and put in a large spoonful of the batter, spreading it over the iron with a palette knife or spatula. Bake for 2 or 3 minutes on each side until the waffle is golden brown. You can either leave them flat or roll them up lengthwise as soon as you remove them from the iron. They will crisp up as they cool and keep well in air-tight tins.

GOUGNETTES
Yeast Fritters

Before the last war, many peasants in the Périgord and the

Quercy ate very simply in the evenings, a typical meal consisting of soup, a salad and fried potatoes or these fritters. Many were too poor to be able to afford meat once a day, and consequently recipes such as this one were evolved so that they should not go hungry. Much has changed since 1945, but these fritters are still quite often made, especially in the villages of the Quercy.

9 oz flour
2 oz sugar
2 eggs
$\frac{1}{4}$ oz yeast
$1\frac{1}{2}$ tablespoonfuls lukewarm water
  a pinch of salt

Serves 4

Dissolve the yeast in the water. Sift the flour, sugar and salt into a bowl. Add the eggs one by one and the yeast. Knead on a board until you have a smooth dough, then put it to rest in a warm room for $1\frac{1}{2}$ hours. Roll out very thinly into a long narrow rectangle and roll this so that you have a long sausage-shaped piece of dough. Cut into one-inch lengths and deep fry in very hot but not boiling oil until they are a good rich brown all over. Serve very hot, sprinkled with icing sugar.

LES JACQUES
Apple Pancakes

$\frac{1}{4}$ lb flour
2 eggs
$\frac{1}{4}$ pint milk
$\frac{1}{4}$ pint water
2 tablespoonfuls sugar
1 tablespoonful oil

189

1 dessertspoonful rum or brandy
a pinch of salt
1 thin slice of bread
3 medium-sized apples

Serves 4 to 6

Make a batter with the flour, eggs, milk, water, sugar, oil, salt
and the rum or brandy. Leave it to rest for 3 hours. Peel and
slice the apples thinly, remove the crust from the bread and cut
it into cubes. Put the bread to soak for a few minutes in the
batter. Heat and grease the frying pan with a very small amount
of oil and pour in a ladleful of the bread and batter mixture.
Tilt the pan so that it spreads out. Put the apples on top of the
batter and then pour another layer of batter over them. Cook for
2 or 3 minutes and then turn or toss the pancake. Cook for
another 2 or 3 minutes so that the apples and underside are
cooked through.

Slide out on to a warm dish, sprinkle over with a little castor
sugar and serve immediately. Sometimes these pancakes are
flambéed on being brought to table with a little rum or brandy
warmed over a flame, touched with a lighted match and then
poured over. The quantities given make two large pancakes,
each one serving two or three.

GATEAU DE CHATAIGNES
Chestnut Cake

2 lb sweetened chestnut purée or 2 lb tin
crème de marrons
2 oz butter
3 eggs
3 oz sugar
2 tablespoonfuls water

Decoration
$\frac{1}{4}$ pint whipped cream
angelica
walnuts

Serves 4 to 6

Beat the chestnut purée in a bowl until it is perfectly smooth. Stir in the egg yolks one by one and the softened butter. Fold in the stiffly beaten egg whites. Lightly oil a round cake tin. Make a caramel with the sugar and water and coat the bottom and sides of the tin with it. Pour in the chestnut batter and cook in a moderate oven, Gas 4/5—355°/375°F, for 1 hour. Turn out when cool.

Coat the top and sides of the cake with the cream and decorate with the angelica and the nuts.

LA BUCHE AUX MARRONS
Chestnut Log

Recipe from Madame Fournier, Campagne, Dordogne

$4\frac{1}{2}$ oz plain chocolate
$4\frac{1}{2}$ oz unsalted butter
$4\frac{1}{2}$ oz sugar
1 lb chestnut purée
1 tablespoonful rum, brandy or strong black coffee

Serves 6

Melt the chocolate with the liquid in a bowl over a pan of hot water. Cream the butter and sugar together and mix them with the chestnut purée and melted chocolate. Spread the mixture out on to a Swiss roll tin lined with aluminium or tin foil, cover with another piece of oiled foil and chill overnight.

Next day, remove the top piece of foil and roll the chestnut mixture up carefully. Trim the edges and decorate with tiny rosettes of meringue made by beating one egg white until stiff, sprinkling over one tablespoonful of icing sugar and beating again for 2 or 3 more minutes. Fill an icing bag with the mixture and pipe the rosettes on to a lightly oiled baking sheet—they should be no larger than half an inch. Bake in a very slow oven, Gas $\frac{1}{2}$—265°F, for 20 minutes. Chill in the refrigerator until ready to serve and hand cream round separately with the log.

GATEAU DE RHUM CAMILLE
Rum Cake

The little café restaurant at Celles, a small village not far from Riberac in the Dordogne, is run by a family of remarkable cooks. Madame takes your order the day before, discussing your meal with you over a leisurely drink. Then she consults Maman, a little round old lady, aged about eighty but still full of vigour and life, who does most of the cooking, which conforms strictly to the rules of old Périgord. But if you decide on a cake or pastry for a sweet, Madame's fifteen-year-old daughter Camille is brought into the discussion. This is one of Camille's specialities. She calls it a rum baba, but as the true baba is made with a yeast dough, I have named the cake after her.

$\qquad$ 3 eggs
$\qquad$ 4½ oz sugar
$\qquad$ ½ oz vanilla sugar
$\qquad$ 4½ oz flour
$\qquad$ 3½ oz butter
$\qquad$ 1 teaspoonful baking powder

Syrup

>4 oz sugar
>scant ½ pint water
>¼ pint rum

Serves 6

Beat together the eggs and the sugars until they are thick and pale lemon in colour. Sift the flour with the baking powder and fold in alternately with the barely melted butter. Pour into a buttered and floured ring mould and bake for 25 minutes in a moderate oven, Gas 4/5—355°/375°F. Do not open the oven door to take a look or the cake may collapse. Turn out on to a cake dish, prick it all over with a fork and spoon over the syrup while the cake is still hot. It should absorb it all.

For the syrup, bring the water and sugar to the boil and add the rum. Boil for 3 minutes and pour over the cake.

LE SOLOGNOT
Chocolate Orange and Hazelnut Mousse

>10 oz bitter chocolate
>5 oz unsalted butter
>2 oz castor sugar
>3 dessertspoonfuls milk
>3 eggs and 1 extra egg white
>2 oz hazelnuts
>8 oz chunky marmalade
>5 tablespoonfuls rum
>24 sponge fingers

Serves 6

Put the nuts in a baking tin in a fairly hot oven for about 8 minutes, rub off the skins and halve them. Heat the marmalade with the rum until it is dissolved and dip the sponge fingers into it. Lightly oil a cylindrical metal mould, about 6 inches in diameter, and line the sides with sponge fingers. Dissolve the chocolate in the milk and add it to the butter, previously creamed with the sugar. Beat in the egg yolks one by one and then stir in the nuts. Add the remaining marmalade (with the chunky pieces of orange), the rum and then the stiffly beaten egg whites. Pour into the mould and chill until set. Turn out just before serving on to a flat dish.

LES CHATAIGNES BLANCHIES
Blanched Chestnuts

Chestnut trees grow all over the Dordogne and Lot Departements of France and nearly every farmer has small chestnut and oak woods on his property. Châtaignes are the chestnuts from the ungrafted trees and are consequently slightly smaller and flatter than marrons, but the flavour is almost the same. *Les châtaignes blanchies* are eaten in the autumn and winter all over the region.

> 2-3 lb chestnuts
> ½ lb old potatoes
> 1 large or two medium sized cabbage
>   leaves
> 1 large handful of aniseed (optional)

Score the chestnuts across the rounded side and roast them in the oven for 15 minutes at Gas 3—335°F. Remove the skins with a small pointed knife. Rinse the chestnuts. Put the potatoes, peeled and cut into slices, in the bottom of a large cocotte or marmite. Blanch the cabbage in salted water for a few minutes to soften the leaves, put a layer over the potatoes, add the chestnuts and place the rest of the cabbage leaves on top. Scatter the aniseed over them and add a very little water, just enough to prevent the potatoes from catching. Cover and cook gently for $1\frac{1}{2}$ hours or until the chestnuts are tender.

Gathering chestnuts

They are eaten plain, with butter, or with a little sugar sprinkled over them, or accompanied by a bowl of hot sweetened milk, and always washed down with wine—usually the young wine of the year, but sometimes, if there are guests, a sweet white wine. In the Dordogne, where fig trees are very common, their leaves replace the cabbage.

195

LES CRUCHADES
Cornmeal Cakes

1¾ pints water
1 oz butter or goose fat
1 lb fine cornmeal
8 oz castor sugar
    grated rind of two lemons
    flour and oil

Serves 4 to 6

Bring the water and the butter or goose fat to the boil in a large pan and then add the cornmeal gradually, stirring constantly to avoid lumps. Add the castor sugar and the grated lemon rind and cook over a low flame, stirring with a wooden spoon, for 15 to 20 minutes. The spoon should then stand upright in the mixture. Turn out on to flat dishes and leave to cool. Cut into slices or rounds about the size of a teacup, roll in flour and fry until golden on each side in a very little oil. Serve, sprinkled over with more sugar.

CARAMELS DE CHOCOLAT
Chocolate Caramels

2 oz chocolate
2 oz butter
2 oz sugar
2 oz honey

Serves 4

Warm together the honey, butter and chocolate in a bowl over boiling water. Add the sugar, mix well and leave for 3 hours.

Put into a heavy pan, melt slowly, bring to the boil and boil for 15 to 20 minutes. Cool, and drop into little paper cases or on to sheets of foil previously oiled.

LES POMMES DE TERRE BRANTOMOISES
Almond Potatoes

  6 oz stale Madeira cake
  8 oz sugar
  4 oz ground almonds
  2 tablespoonfuls rum or brandy
    the stiffly beaten white of 1 large egg
    cocoa
10 whole blanched almonds, cut in fine slivers

Serves 4 to 6

Grate the cake finely into a bowl. Add the sugar, mix well, and then add the ground almonds and the rum or brandy. Finally stir in the beaten egg white. Form into balls the size of medium to small potatoes. Roll each one in the cocoa and stick the almond slivers into them all over.

Chapter Five

SAUCES AND DRINKS

SAUCES

GELEE POUR ASPIC
Basic Aspic Jelly

1 veal bone
2 pig's trotters or a calf's foot
8 oz shin of beef
  a poultry carcase, if possible
2 onions, each stuck with a clove
2 carrots
  a large bouquet garni of thyme, parsley
  and bayleaf
4 or 5 peppercorns

Put all the ingredients into a large pan, cover with water and bring to the boil. Skim and then simmer very gently for at least 4 hours, with the lid of the pan tilted. Turn up the heat and boil hard to reduce the liquid. Turn it into a bowl through a strainer and leave till next day. Remove every speck of fat, which should have set at the top of the jelly. To clarify the jelly, you will need one egg white and the crushed shell per quart of liquid. Put the jelly into a large pan over a gentle heat, beat up the egg white to a froth and add it and the shell to the melting jelly, beating it in with a wooden spoon. Bring very gently to almost boiling point (the liquid should barely shudder) and keep it at this temperature for 10 minutes. Then turn off the heat and leave the pan for another 10 minutes.

Line a colander or fine mesh salad or egg basket with a piece of muslin, making sure the material is securely tied to the handles. Hang this, or a jelly bag if you have one, over a large bowl and very carefully pour the contents of the pan through it, being careful to disturb the crust which has formed at the top as little as possible. Leave it to drip without squeezing or stirring. The liquid should be beautifully clear and is now ready to be flavoured with Madeira, white wine, sherry or whatever flavouring you are using. Allow a tablespoonful of Madeira or sherry and three of white wine for every three or four pints of liquid.

LA MARINADE
Marinade

A marinade is a highly flavoured liquid in which food is steeped for some time in order to flavour and soften the fibres and so tenderise tough meat. It is usually made of herbs, wine and vegetables, but there are many variations. The following is a basic marinade for beef and game, such as hare.

199

1 bottle **red wine**
4 tablespoonfuls olive oil
1 sliced carrot
1 sliced onion
2 crushed cloves garlic
  a piece of orange or lemon peel
1 teaspoonful crushed juniper berries
  a pinch of nutmeg
2 sprigs each of thyme and parsley
2 crushed bayleaves
  salt and freshly ground black pepper
  or 6 crushed peppercorns
2 tablespoonfuls brandy (optional)

Mix all the ingredients together and pour the marinade over the meat in a glass or china bowl. Cover and leave to steep for 6 to 12 hours or according to the recipe, turning the meat from time to time.

COURT BOUILLON

$\frac{1}{2}$ pint water
$\frac{1}{2}$ pint dry white wine
  or $\frac{3}{4}$ pint water and a good dash of dry white vermouth
1 onion stuck with a clove
1 carrot
  a bouquet garni
6 peppercorns
  salt

Bring all the ingredients to the boil, simmer for 25 minutes and strain. For a more concentrated fish stock or *fumet*, add fish bones and trimmings to the above ingredients and reduce by a third after the initial 25 minute simmering.

LA SAUCE AUX CORNICHONS
Gherkin Sauce

1 oz butter
1 oz flour
$\frac{1}{4}$ pint white wine
$\frac{1}{2}$ pint water
1 small lump of sugar
1 egg yolk
1 small onion
2 tablespoonfuls finely chopped gherkins

Serves 3 to 4

Buy the sharp tasting gherkins of the type sold as cocktail gherkins. Chop the onion finely and soften it in the butter. Sprinkle over the flour and simmer until the mixture is a pale gold in colour. Add the wine and water gradually and the sugar lump. Season with salt and pepper, cover and simmer for 45 minutes with an asbestos mat under the pan. Beat up a little of the sauce with the egg yolk and thicken with this liaison. Finally stir in the gherkins. This sauce is good with boiled ham.

SAUCE ESPAGNOLE, SAUCE MADERE and SAUCE PERIGUEUX
Spanish Sauce, Madeira Sauce and Périgueux Sauce

Sauce Espagnole is the foundation for many sauces, such as

P   201

Madeira Sauce. It will keep in the refrigerator for several days and is a most useful sauce to have on hand.

> 2 finely sliced carrots
> 3 or 4 chopped shallots
> 2 tablespoonfuls chopped ham or lean gammon
> 2 oz mushroom stalks or peelings
> 3 oz butter
> 2 oz flour
> 2 tablespoonfuls tomato purée
> 1 bayleaf
> 2 sprigs each of thyme and parsley
> $\frac{1}{4}$ pint white wine
> 3 pints good stock

Madeira Sauce

> $\frac{1}{4}$ pint Madeira
> 1 oz butter

Serves 4

Brown the carrots, shallots and ham carefully in the butter. Add the sifted flour and cook slowly, stirring constantly until it turns a deep golden brown, and not letting it burn. Add the hot stock, wine, tomato purée, mushroom stalks or peelings, bayleaf, thyme and parsley. Simmer for $2\frac{1}{2}$ hours, skimming carefully as the fat and scum rise to the top. Strain through a fine sieve.

For Madeira sauce, take one pint of the Spanish sauce, reduced by a third and add $\frac{1}{4}$ pint Madeira. Simmer just below boiling for 5 minutes and then, off the fire, beat in one ounce of butter cut into tiny pieces.

The addition of sliced truffles, 2 or 3 minutes towards the end of the cooking time for the Madeira sauce makes a Périgueux sauce.

SAUCE PERIGUEUX
Périgueux Sauce

Recipe from Madame Dumonteil's

1 veal bone sawn into two or three pieces
1 medium onion, sliced
2 chopped shallots
1 clove garlic
1 sliced carrot
2 sprigs thyme
2 bayleaves
2 cloves
1 tablespoonful flour
1 tablespoonful butter
1 tablespoonful tomato purée
1 glass white wine
2 pints beef or veal stock
2 tablespoonfuls cognac
4 tablespoonfuls Madeira
2 oz very small button mushrooms
2 or 3 truffles

Serves 4 to 6

Put the veal bone, onion, garlic, carrot, thyme, bayleaves and cloves in a baking dish and brown in the oven for 40 minutes. Melt the butter in a large casserole, add the flour and cook for 2 or 3 minutes. Put in the contents of the baking dish and add the tomato purée, white wine and stock. Season with pepper and leave to simmer on top of an asbestos mat for 4 hours. Strain the sauce into a clean pan, reduce by a third and add the cognac, Madeira and mushrooms, previously simmered in a tablespoonful of butter and a little water until just tender. Simmer for 2 or 3 minutes and then add the truffles, cut into slices. Simmer just below boiling point for another 3 minutes.

This makes a very good Périgueux sauce, but takes up a lot of time. A simpler and quicker version:

SAUCE PERIGUEUX
Périgueux Sauce

Recipe from Monsieur Curnonsky's

This version is included in *The Traditional Recipes of the Provinces of France.*

Although some cooks stipulate a dry white wine for it, one old Périgourdine lady, well known in her village for the food she used to produce at weddings and banquets, told me that for Curnonsky's recipe she always uses a Monbazillac or medium sweet wine.

3 shallots
1 onion
2 oz goose or pork fat
1 pint good stock
5 oz white wine
4 tablespoonfuls brandy
1 tablespoonful flour
3 or 4 truffles

Serves 4

Chop the shallots and fry to a pale gold in half the fat. Add the wine and the warmed brandy and set it alight. In a separate pan, fry the finely sliced onion in the rest of the fat until it is softened and has taken on a little colour. Add the flour and simmer for 2 minutes and then add the warmed stock. Mix the two sauces together and leave the mixture for 2 hours either on a very low heat with an asbestos mat under the pan or at the side of the stove. Stir frequently. Strain the sauce and add the truffle peelings to cook in the sauce for a few minutes, then add the sliced truffles and simmer without boiling for another 5 minutes.

SAUCE VINAIGRETTE AUX OEUFS
Egg Sauce with Vinegar

This, which is simple to make, is one of the standby sauces for hors d'oeuvres, fish, cold meats, boiled beef and chicken.

> 1 shallot or spring onion
> 2 tablespoonfuls parsley, finely chopped
> 1 tablespoonful chives, finely chopped
> a few tarragon leaves when available, finely chopped
> 1 clove garlic
> 4 tablespoonfuls olive oil
> 1 tablesponful vinegar
> 1 egg boiled for 3 minutes

Serves 4

Chop the shallot or spring onion and the garlic together until almost reduced to a purée. Add the vinegar and the oil, season with salt and pepper and stir in the herbs. Mix in the egg yolk and the chopped egg white just before serving. The sauce should not be too thin.

205

SAUCE VERTE de PERIGORD
Périgourdine Green Sauce

2 hard-boiled eggs
2 small spring onions
  a dessertspoonful each of chervil, chives
  and parsley
1 clove garlic
  a teaspoonful yellow French mustard
1 tablespoonful vinegar
4 fluid oz olive oil

Serves 4

Sieve the hard-boiled eggs and then pound them to a paste in a mortar with the garlic. Add the mustard, the vinegar and then the oil, as for a mayonnaise. Finally stir in the very finely chopped spring onions, using both the white and green parts, and the other herbs. Season with salt and pepper.

This is a sauce which tends to separate and curdle easily, so don't make it too long beforehand. It is usually served with fish, hot or cold boiled meats and poultry.

SAUCE AUX OIGNONS DE PERIGORD
Onion Sauce

24 pickling or silverskin onions
 3 oz finely diced gammon
 1 tablespoonful goose or pork fat
 1 tablespoonful flour
 1 pint clear meat stock

1 dessertspoonful chopped parsley
a pinch of nutmeg
a few drops of lemon juice or vinegar
a bouqet garni of thyme and a bayleaf

Serves 4

Fry the onions in the fat until golden, add the gammon and continue frying for a few minutes. Sprinkle the flour over it and when it has taken on a little colour add the stock, the parsley, the bouquet garni, salt and pepper. Simmer very gently for 45 minutes. Just before serving, add the nutmeg and the lemon juice or vinegar.

SAUCE AU ROQUEFORT ET AUX NOIX
Roquefort and Walnut Sauce

4 oz roquefort cheese
1 oz finely chopped walnuts
1 medium sized cold boiled potato
1 egg yolk
$\frac{1}{4}$ pint olive oil or walnut oil
1 teaspoonful chopped parsley
a squeeze of lemon

Serves 4

Put the cheese through a sieve and then cream it with the egg yolk and the mashed potato. Add the olive oil or walnut oil drop by drop, as for a mayonnaise. Season with pepper and stir in the chopped walnuts and the parsley. Finish off the sauce with a squeeze of lemon.

207

DRINKS

VIN DE CASSIS
Blackcurrant Wine

1 lb blackcurrants
12 fluid oz water
7 oz preserving sugar
1¾ pints brandy
2 blackcurrant leaves

Makes approximately 2½ pints

Bruise the leaves and put them with the fruit into a large jar or stone crock, cover with the brandy and leave to macerate for 3 months. If you can expose the jar to the rays of the sun, so much the better. Strain and press all the juice out of the fruit, and put through a filter. Dissolve the sugar in the water, boil for 10 minutes and add when cold.

LA LIQUEUR DE COINGS
Quince Liqueur

10 lb very ripe quinces
¼ pint brandy for every pint of juice and pulp
½ lb sugar   }
¾ pint water   } for every quart of liquid

Wipe the bloom from the quinces, wash and dry them. Grate them (including the peel) into a bowl and add the brandy. Leave to rest for 3 days and then strain, pressing out as much of the juice as possible. Make a syrup of the sugar and the water,

208

cool it and add it to the liquid. Filter into bottles, cork down
and leave for at least 6 months before drinking.

LA LIQUEUR DE LAIT
Milk Liqueur

Here is an oddity. When I first came across it, I could not
believe that the clear golden liquid I was drinking was in any
way connected with milk. But I was assured that milk consti-
tuted one of its principal ingredients and that it was a very old
Périgourdine recipe.

$3\frac{1}{2}$ pints fresh full cream milk
$1\frac{1}{2}$ bottles brandy
2 lb sugar lumps
4 vanilla sticks
2 unpeeled oranges, sliced
4 unpeeled lemons, sliced

Makes approximately 3 pints

Put all the ingredients together in a large glass jar or stone
crock and stir every day for 40 days with a wooden spoon (the
original recipe stipulated a peeled hazelnut twig). Strain
through a fine muslin and then filter carefully. I use coffee
filter papers or bags, and you will need large ones at least 8in in
diameter, fitted inside a wide plastic funnel. Bottle and leave
for 6 months before drinking.

BROU DE NOIX
Walnut Liqueur

50 green walnuts
1 cinnamon stick

209

4 cloves
1 blade of mace
thinly pared rind of a lemon
preserving sugar
$2\frac{1}{2}$ pints vodka or pure white spirit

Makes approximately $2\frac{1}{2}$ pints

The nuts must be gathered in June when they are green and still tender enough to be pierced with a darning needle. Cut them in half and discard the centre piece. Pound them in a mortar until they are reduced to a pulp and then put them in a glass jar or stone crock. Add the spices, lemon rind and vodka, cover and leave for 6 weeks, in the sun if possible. Strain through a muslin, pressing out as much juice as possible, and add 4oz sugar for every pint of liquid. Leave for another 7 to

10 days, by which time the sugar should have dissolved, then put through a filter and bottle.

Peach Leaf Aperitif

120 peach leaves
  6 fluid oz pure white spirit
    or $\frac{1}{2}$ pint brandy
  2 bottles white wine
 40 sugar lumps
  1 cinnamon stick
  4 cloves

Makes approximately 3 pints

Macerate the peach leaves in the wine and spices for 4 days. Strain and add the sugar and alcohol to the liquid, stirring well until the sugar is dissolved. Bottle and leave for 7 days before drinking. This aperitif, one of the most common in the area, can also be made with red wine.

PRUNEAUX AU VIN BLANC
Prunes in White Wine

1 lb Californian prunes
1$\frac{1}{2}$ bottles medium sweet white wine
$\frac{1}{2}$ lb lump sugar
6 fluid oz brandy

Put the prunes into a large glass jar, cover with the white wine and let them soak in it for 10 days. Keep the jar covered. Top up with more white wine as the prunes absorb it, ensuring that the liquid covers the fruit by at least half an inch the whole time. Strain the juice and add the sugar. Dissolve over a low heat, bring to the boil, skim and boil for 3 minutes. When completely cold, add the brandy and pour over the prunes. Cover and leave for at least 6 weeks before using.

Chapter Six

THE FETES

DESPITE all the hard work the people of the Périgord and the Quercy still find time to enjoy themselves, and nowhere more than at the local fêtes, which are held in nearly every village and town. Sometimes these are very small, involving a few decorated floats on a local theme (generally agricultural), a merry-go-round and dodgem cars; sometimes they are more elaborate. Often they include torchlight processions round the village, such as one I attended where the local Mayor, a communist like so many in the south and south-west, had engaged a troup of majorettes dressed in white with scarlet cloaks and hats. They led the procession, carrying their torches and lanterns and singing the Internationale, which seemed slightly incongruous in the beautiful old village famed for its château and church. Nobody took the political overtones seriously—least of all the owner of the château and the local priest, both of whom graced the occasion with their presence.

After the procession, everybody rushed to the marquees

where dinner was served on long trestle tables, and the evening ended with dancing and fireworks. On this occasion the firework display was good, but it is not always so. At the very small fêtes one often has to stand and wait a long time for the next lot of fireworks to be set off; yet they never fail to draw loud oohs and gasps from the patient crowd. Often these fêtes have purely local traditions, peculiar to the villages or towns themselves, such as at Gourdon in the Lot where the fête always takes place on the first Sunday after Midsummer's Eve. There the procession included a number of penitents dressed in blue and in white followed by a young lamb, crowned with multi-coloured ribbons and led by the statue of St John the Baptist, patron saint of the town. This custom has now died out, but not

214

far away in another town the musicians who have been chosen to play on the day of the fête accompanied by the local boys still sound the first reveille in front of the houses of the members of the local Municipal Council; they also do it early on New Year's Day, and this is not always very well received after the celebrations of the night before.

One custom common to every village in the Périgord and the Quercy is that which is practised on St John the Baptist's Day. As soon as dusk falls, great bonfires are lit on the hills outside the villages and are blessed by the local priest, who holds a small service there. Afterwards the boys jump over the embers and each girl takes a small burnt twig to put under her pillow that night, when she is supposed to dream of her future husband.

Anyone finding himself in the Dordogne on the first weekend in July should make the effort to go to the Felibrée Périgourdin, which is held on the Sunday. This is the largest of all Périgourdin fêtes and takes place each year in a different town with all the local villages around co-operating in the arrangements. In 1970 it was held in Verteillac, a very small town in the north-west of the Dordogne and capital of a canton. All winter the people in the villages of the canton had been making small paper roses of all colours of the rainbow. These were strung into long garlands and hung across the roads leading into the town, forming gay canopies. Paper roses and coloured lights decorated the trees in the square and more garlands were strung from the top of the church steeple. In the centre of the square men in national costume worked a huge old oil press and a forge, while next to them stood examples of local furniture made of walnut, and a hut of straw shaped like a beehive to represent the local honey industry. The Felibrée is a folklore fête, with the procession (dressed in national costume) led by the Queen of the Périgord, who is chosen from the girls nominated by their villages to participate in the events. The local patois is spoken throughout the proceedings, including the open air Mass, which began the day in Verteillac in the grounds of the local château. The banquet was composed of food and wines of the country served by costumed waiters and waitresses who were, for the most part, local inhabitants, and this was followed by folk dances and songs, many of which are performed only on this day of the year. Despite the fact that an enormous amount of money is spent annually in the preparations for the Felibrée and that it attracts a certain number of tourists, the fête has not become commercial. It still remains a purely Périgourdine affair for the local people, and the organisers and participants take great care to keep it that way.

APPENDICES

STOCKISTS AND SUPPLIERS

London
For people living in London, shopping for Continental products like those mentioned in this book presents little difficulty.
The large London stores all have good ranges of most of them,
and these stores also have mail order services. In addition, a visit
to the specialist shops of Soho and to the fruit and vegetable markets of Berwick Street and Rupert Street will usually provide
what is needed. Among the shops well stocked from the point
of view of these recipes are the following:

John Barker & Co Ltd, Kensington High Street, W8
Elizabeth David, 46 Bourne Street, SW1
Justin R. de Blank, 42b Elizabeth Street, SW1
Fortnum & Mason Ltd, 181 Piccadilly, W1
Harrods Ltd, Knightsbridge, SW1
Jacksons of Piccadilly, 171 Piccadilly, W1
Randall & Aubin Ltd, 16 Brewer Street, W1
Louis Roche Ltd, 14 Old Compton Street, W1
Selfridges Ltd, Oxford Street, W1
Truffes, Beauchamp Place, SW3

Provinces
The large London stores have mail order services which will
send goods to provincial customers, and the following are a few

of the provincial shops which sell products required for these recipes:

Bath, Somerset: *Caters of Bath*

Birmingham, Warwickshire: *Fish and Vegetable Market*, The Bullring
Rackhams of Birmingham

Bournemouth, Hampshire: *Jacksons*, 37-41 Seamoor Road

Brighton, Sussex: *Country Style*, Ship Street

Bristol, Gloucestershire: *Sargesons*, The Mall, Clifton
Charles Saunders, Baldwin Street

Bury St Edmunds, Suffolk: *Thomas Ridley & Son*, Abbeygate Street

Cheltenham, Gloucestershire: *Cavendish House*, Promenade

Chichester, Sussex: *Epicure*, Crane Street

Colchester, Essex: *F. Spearing & Son*, Dedham

Gloucester: *Gourmet Store*, The Market
Also the Market for fish

Hitchin, Hertfordshire: *Halsey & Sons*, Market Place

Lewes, Sussex: *The Gourmet Delicatessen*, 18 High Street

Nottingham: *Burtons of Nottingham*

Ombersley, Worcestershire: *Evertons*, Worcester Road

St Albans, Hertfordshire: *Jacksons*, 9 George Street

Salisbury, Wiltshire: *Robert Stokes*

Stourbridge, Worcestershire: *The Delicatesserie*, 146 High Street

Sutton Coldfield, Warwickshire: *Prana Wholefoods*, 30 Birmingham Road

Tunbridge Wells, Kent: *Jacksons*, 37 Mount Ephraim

Worcester: *Grays*, Bath Road

Wales

Cardiff: *James Howell*, Wharton Street

Monmouth: *Kitchener*, 11 Agincourt Square

218

Scotland

Edinburgh: *Valvona & Crolla,* 19 Elm Row
 Young & Saunders, 5 Queensferry Street

Orange-flower water and aniseed water can be bought from most large chemists throughout the country; aniseed grains from Indian and Oriental food shops; and fresh yeast, herbs and spices from health food stores.

COMPARATIVE COOKERY MEASURES

Unusual British measures are included where they correspond to standard metric measures.

Solid Measures

British	American	Metric (approximate)
1oz	1oz (2 tablespoons)	30 grammes
4½oz	4½oz	125 grammes (un quart)
½lb butter (8oz)	1 cup	
½lb caster sugar	1 cup and 2 tablespoons	
½lb flour	2 cups and 1 tablespoon	
9oz	9oz	250 grammes (½ livre)
1lb (16oz)	1lb (16oz)	454 grammes
1lb butter	2 cups	
1lb caster sugar	2⅓ cups	
1lb flour	Just under 4½ cups	
1lb 1½oz	1lb 1½oz	500 grammes (1 livre)
2lb 3oz	2lb 3oz	1 kilogramme

Liquid Measures

British	American	Metric (approximate)
1 teaspoon	1¼ teaspoons	6cc
1 tablespoon	1¼ tablespoons	16cc
5 fluid oz (1 gill, ¼ pint)	½ cup and 1 dessertspoon	1.46 décilitres
6 fluid oz	½ cup and 2 tablespoons	1.751 décilitres (1 verre)
10 fluid oz (½ pint)	1¼ cups	2.86 décilitres
20 fluid oz (1 pint)	2½ cups (1¼ pints)	5.71 décilitres
35 fluid oz (1¾ pints)	2 pints	1 litre
1 quart (2 pints)	2½ pints	1.142 litres
1 gallon (8 pints)	10 pints	4.571 litres

The British pint is equivalent to 20 fluid oz.

The American pint equals 16 fluid oz.

The British standard measuring cup equals 10 fluid oz.

The American standard measuring cup equals 8 fluid oz.

1 litre = 2 demilitres = 10 décilitres = 100 centilitres = 1,000 millilitres.

TABLE OF OVEN SETTINGS AND TEMPERATURES

Electricity Degrees Fahrenheit	Electricity Degrees Centigrade	Gas Oven Thermostat Settings	
240	116	$\frac{1}{4}$	Very slow
265	130	$\frac{1}{2}$	
290	143	1	Slow
310	154	2	
335	168	3	Moderate
355	179	4	
375	190	5	Moderately hot
400	205	6	
425	218	7	Hot
445	229	8	
470	243	9	Very hot
490	253	10	
510	265	11	
525	274	12	

People with Natural Gas Cookers may experience some difficulty in simmering on top of the stove, in which case an asbestos mat placed under the pan will help to reduce the heat.

BIBLIOGRAPHY

English Books

Britain's Wild Larder: Fungi by Claire Loewenfeld (Faber & Faber)

The Generous Earth by Philip Oyler (Hodder & Stoughton)

Sons of the Generous Earth by Philip Oyler (Hodder & Stoughton)

Mushrooms and Toadstools by John Ramsbottom (William Collins)

Books Translated into English

Larousse Gastronomique edited by Nina Froud and Charlotte Turgeon (Hamlyn Publishing Group)

The Traditional Recipes of France edited by Curnonsky (W. H. Allen)

French Books

La Guyenne, l'Aquitaine et la Gascogne (Editions Arthaud, Paris)

Les Plats Régionnaux de France by Austin de Croze (Editions Montaigne, Paris)

La France Gourmande by Fulbert Dumonteil (Librairie Universelle, Paris)

Mon Périgord by A. de Lacrousille

La Bonne Cuisine de Périgord by La Mazille (Flammarion, Paris)

Le Lot a Petites Journées (Editions Meyzenc, Cahore)

Les Bons Plats de France by Pampille (A. Fayard, Paris)

L'Art due Bien Manger by Edmond Richardin (Editions d'Art et de Littérature, Paris)

Le Périgord by Jean Secret

Le Vieux Quercy by Chanoine Eugene Sol (Bibliothèque de la Maison des Oeuvres, Cahors)

222

ACKNOWLEDGEMENTS

I SHOULD like to thank the many people who have so kindly and generously helped me to gather information for this book and who have encouraged me to write it. Among them are the following: Monsieur and Madame Bujan of the *Hotel de Tout Va Bien* at Valence d'Agen; Dr. and Madame Coriat of Paris; Monsieur and Madame Courregelongue of the *Hotel Prune d'Or* at Villeneuve sur Lot; Madame Dumonteil of the *Truffe de Périgord Charcuterie* in Riberac; Monsieur and Madame Marty of the *Boucherie et Charcuterie* in Nanteuil de Bourzac; Monsieur Raymond Oliver, proprietor of the *Grand Vefour* restaurants in Paris and London, Master Chef and author of many cookery books; Monsieur Jean Rougier of the *Maison Rougier* at Calviac; and Madame Lucienne Touren in Cordes. I owe a special debt of gratitude to Monsieur Pierre Escorbiac of Cahors, who devoted so much of his time to giving me invaluable advice from his great knowledge of the regional cookery of this part of France; and to my neighbours Monsieur and Madame Vincent of La Haute Valade, who let me try out many recipes in their home, for their kindness and encouragement.

I should also like to make sincere acknowledgement to the many organisations that have helped me in my search for information. They include: Messrs W. H. Allen & Co of London, who gave me permission to reproduce two recipes from their *Traditional Recipes of the Provinces of France*, edited by Curnonsky; the Director of Beyne Frères in Eymet de Périgord, who allowed me to take some of the recipes from their very interesting booklet; the Directrice and staff of the Municipal Library of Périgueux, who have patiently dealt with my enquiries and obtained old manuscripts and out of print books for me.

GENERAL INDEX

225

INDEX OF RECIPES
(In French)